J   535833
358.4   12.95
Mus
Musciano
Corsair aces

DATE DUE			

To Mary Lou
With Love and Pride

Corsair Aces
The Bent-Wing Bird
Over the Pacific
2nd Edition

Walter A. Musciano

AERO
A division of TAB BOOKS Inc.
Blue Ridge Summit, PA

SECOND EDITION
Copyright © 1979, 1989 by Walter A. Musciano
FIRST PRINTING

Published 1979 by Arco Publishing Company, Inc.
219 Park Avenue South,
New York, N.Y. 10003
All Rights Reserved

Library of Congress Cataloging-in-Publication Data:

Musciano, Walter A.
    Corsair aces : the bent-wing bird over the Pacific / by Walter A. Musciano. — 2nd ed.
        p. cm.
    Bibliography: p.
    Includes index.
    ISBN 0-8306-8269-4 (pbk.)
    1. World War, 1939-1945—Aerial operations, American. 2. World War, 1939-1945—Naval operations, American. 3. World War, 1939-1945—Campaigns—Pacific Area. 4. Fighter pilots—United States—Biography. 5. United States. Navy—Biography. 6. United States. Marine Corps—Biography. 7. Corsair (Fighter planes) I. Title.
    D790.M87   1989
    940.54′26′0922—dc20   89-6736
                                                          CIP

Jeff Worsinger: Acquisitions Editor
Steven H. Mesner: Technical Editor
Katherine Brown: Production

Contents

Acknowledgments   *vii*

Foreword   *viii*

Introduction   *ix*

Chapter 1   The Weapon: The Vought
             F4U Corsair   *1*

Chapter 2   The Battleground: Through the
             Solomons to Victory   *25*

Chapter 3   The Men: Corsair Aces
             Make History   *47*
             Kenneth A. Walsh—Donald N. Aldrich—Harold L.
             Spears—Robert M. Hanson—Wilbur J. Thomas—
             Harold E. Segal—Gregory Boyington—Ira C.
             Kepford

Chapter 4   Korea: Night Ace   *99*

Appendix A   Fighter Organization and
              Squadron Histories   *109*

Appendix B   Corsair Targets and Losses during
              World War II   *117*

Appendix C   Vought F4U Corsair Development
              during World War II   *118*

Appendix D   Decorations and Awards   *119*

Index   *130*

Acknowledgments

The author expresses his sincere thanks to:

Arthur L. Schoeni and Ling-Temco-Vought
Colonel T. P. O'Callaghan and the United States Marine Corps
Commander D. K. Dagle and the United States Navy
Albert L. Lewis and *Air Progress* Magazine
D. C. MacMillan, John W. Fair,
  and the American Fighter Aces Association
Presidential Assistant Benjamin W. Fridge
U. S. Information Agency
U. S. National Archives
Henry Tremont
A. E. Ferko
Lt. Col. Kenneth Walsh USMC (Ret.)
N. H. Hauprich
Diane M. Jenkins
Col. O. Keith Williams USMC (Ret.)

for their kind assistance, which made this volume possible.

Foreword

Walter Musciano has done a fine job in writing *Corsair Aces*. The men, the plane, the places bring to surface memories that will never die. He tells of the first Corsairs to land at Guadalcanal on 12 February 1943, but he doesn't know how the other pilots envied those lucky pilots of VMF 124.

All the other squadrons were flying the F4F Wildcat, which was just as rugged as the Corsair, but some 70 knots slower. However, it wasn't long until we were all equipped with the Corsair, and we started up the Solomon Islands chain, ready to eat the Japs' lunch.

All the living aces listed in the book are in their seventies or soon will be. We miss the flying, the excitement, and friendships . . . all but the dying. Thank you, Walter, for reminding us we are *Marines*, and we're out in front.

O. K. Williams
Lt. Col. USMCR (Rtd.)
1 August 1988

Introduction

This book is about men—brave men who fought with outstanding valor and unselfish devotion for their country. Some gave their lives for a cause they believed to be just while others were more fortunate and were spared. All fought well and all earned the undying gratitude of a proud nation.

The men you are about to meet have even more in common with each other: All are aces; all are Americans; and all are superb fighter pilots. All fought the finest fighter pilots that the enemy had to offer and yet they managed to break the back of the cream of enemy air power.

There is still another important common denominator that can be applied to these warriors: They all used the same basic weapon with which to batter the enemy, the Vought F4U Corsair.

In few other campaigns in the history of warfare has the fighter plane played an equally important role as the Corsair did during the year of 1943 in the South Pacific Theatre of Operations. With these intrepid men at the controls, the Corsair made its operational debut during the Solomon Islands campaign and flashed through the sky wreaking such havoc on its Japanese opponents that, in the end, it remained alone—the victor in a hard won battle.

The Corsair and its intrepid pilots did not rest upon the laurels earned in the South Pacific victories, but continued into the Central Pacific to the shores of the Japanese Empire itself.

Once again, the Corsair and its pilots performed yeoman service in action during the Korean War, operating from carriers as well as land bases until the armistice in 1953.

1

The Weapon
The Vought F4U Corsair

The Vought F4U Corsair, ideally suited to both defensive as well as offensive roles, was the perfect weapon for the island-hopping strategy employed in the Solomons. After repelling the early Japanese raids down the "Slot," the Corsair became the escort for United States Army heavy bombers. It fitted in smoothly with the Army escort fighters due to its superior performance at intermediate altitudes. With the bombers normally flying at 20,000 feet, the low-flying Curtiss P-40 afforded little protection from the higher-flying Zero. The twin-engined Lockheed P-38 Lightning, on the other hand, was more at home at altitudes above 30,000 feet.

With the advent of the Corsair, a standard escort pattern was developed for the increasingly larger bombing raids directed against Rabaul. The big bombers lumbered along at 20,000 feet with the P-40 providing low protection and the P-38 supplying top cover. The Marine Corsairs flew between 20,000 and 30,000 feet in loose staggered formation with four to eight airplanes per layer. Weaving over an area two to four miles wide, the F4U could give immediate protection to the bombers. Because the intercepting Japanese fighters invariably went directly for the egg-laying giants, the Corsair pilots were usually the first to engage the Zeroes, often with the odds very much in favor of the enemy. That the Corsair in the hands of a skillful pilot was more than a match for the best Japan could offer was quickly demonstrated. A closer look at this unusual fighter will help explain why it remained in first-line service longer than any other fighter ever built.

Designed in 1938 and flown in 1940, the Corsair first tasted combat at Guadalcanal in early 1943. It soon established aerial superiority over the vaunted Japanese Navy Zero, the highly maneuverable aircraft that had previously outperformed all U.S. fighters. It was the first American fighter to top 400 miles per hour and the first to house a 2,000-horsepower engine. Interrogation of high Japanese brass at the end of the war disclosed the fact they considered the Corsair the most formidable fighter in use by any service in the Pacific.

1

A number of factors must combine to shape the environment in which a military aircraft can reach old age and still remain a first-line weapon. The tactical situation, economics, armament development all play a part. Most important, however, the aircraft itself must be a sound basic design, capable of continual upgrading, and incorporating a reliable powerplant.

The beginning was a Navy design competition issued on February 1, 1938, for a high-performance fighter. Chance Vought responded on April 8, 1938, with a proposal to build the XF4U-1. The heart of the new fighter was to be the huge, untried Pratt and Whitney 2,000-horsepower air-cooled radial engine.

The design was conceived in an unfavorable climate. Under pressure from the Army Air Corps, Pratt and Whitney was being urged to concentrate on liquid-cooled engines, thus putting the R-2800 radial air-cooled design on precarious ground. The Army was convinced that the future of high-speed fighters lay with streamlined shapes developed around in-line liquid-cooled types. Current designs, the P-38 and P-40, promised much, and presented far less drag than a big radial engine such as the proposed R-2800. Pratt and Whitney held that an air-cooled radial was inherently lighter, and that the weight saved was far more important than increased drag. Furthermore, the Navy had always favored radials, and the Corsair was soon to prove that Pratt and Whitney's huge 2,000-horsepower powerplant had what it takes.

In the process of designing a fighter to accommodate the world's most powerful engine, it became necessary to fit the largest propeller ever built to that time, a three-bladed Hamilton-Standard with a diameter of 13 feet 4 inches. To provide the needed clearance for this giant, Vought engineers hit upon the unique configuration that was to stamp the appearance of all the Corsairs to come: the inverted gull wing. This unusual design gave the airplane its nickname, "bent-wing bird."

The beginning. XF4U-1 Corsair prototype flew May 29, 1940 with Vought test pilot Lyman Bullard in the cockpit. First fighter to have a 2,000-hp engine, top speed was 405 mph. (Ling-Temco-Vought Photograph)

But what might seem a large concession in design actually had many other good features. Aerodynamically, a right-angle juncture between wings and fuselage resulted in the lowest possible drag. A much shorter and sturdier landing gear leg was possible. Originally the fuel tanks were in the wings; the engineers wanted to retract the landing gear straight aft and the short leg was needed to fit the available area. Pilot visibility was improved by the lowered wing. And because the fighter was slated for carrier duty, it was limited to folded wing height due to hangar deck restrictions then prevalent.

Limited production was the rule in 1938 and Vought could concentrate on the main objective: design the fastest fighter, rather than worry about mass production. The inverted gull wing structure presented many problems, and thousands of hours were spent on its design alone. With the demand for speed and more speed, aerodynamic cleanliness received tremendous attention. And the radial engine stigma forced close attention to reducing drag in every way to offset the very large frontal area. Fortunately, the engineering staff was given a free hand to pursue every avenue of weight and drag reduction while boosting speed potential.

On June 11, 1938, the Navy awarded Chance Vought a contract to build the first experimental Corsair, the XF4U-1. The specifications called for a single-seat fighter with a service ceiling of at least 27,000 feet. With a contract in hand, work began at once. Even so, the Navy's Bureau of Aeronautics could not inspect the mockup until February 8, 1940. By this time, war seemed much closer, and work was accelerated. Only seven weeks later, on March 29, the XF4U-1 took to the air for the first time with Vought's Chief Pilot, Lyman Bullard, at the controls.

Unique shape of the Corsair is shown in this view of the XF4U-1. Forward location of cockpit was feature of prototype only. Production aircraft had cockpit moved three feet aft, but "window pane" canopy appeared on early run machines. (Ling-Temco-Vought Photograph)

A few days later, with Rear Admiral John Towers, Chief of the Navy's Bureau of Aeronautics, looking on, the Corsair raced through a speed course at 405 miles per hour. Without revealing the actual speed, Admiral Towers told witnesses that they had just seen the most powerful and fastest fighter in America. At a time when 400 miles per hour was almost a mythical figure, the Corsair's performance was ample proof that Pratt and Whitney's faith in the air-cooled engine had paid off. Not long after, Major General Henry H. (Hap) Arnold, Chief of the Army Air Corps, heard about the Corsair's ability. It doubtless influenced his decision to allow Pratt

Clearly shown are two .30-caliber machine guns in cowl. Wing guns were .50-caliber. Ultimate armament eliminated cowl guns in favor of six wing-mounted .50s. Color was overall silver with chrome yellow upper wing surfaces. (Ling-Temco-Vought Photograph)

and Whitney to cancel its liquid-cooled engine contract. At the same time he requested the company to concentrate its energies in the radial field.

Following these test flights, the design was approved with a Navy request for a production proposal on November 28, 1940. The F4U-1 production model to re-place the XF4U-1 incorporated a number of changes. The military requirements that had influenced the internal structure of the experimental model had changed, and the F4U-1 was in for some strenuous revamping.

The engine was changed from the prototype XR-2800-2 to the R-2800-8(B). Integral wing fuel tanks (47 gallons each) were incorporated in the early F4U-1. A CO_2 bottle was provided to purge these wing tanks under combat conditions. Later, the integral fuel tanks were removed from the wing center sections and outer panel leading edges. Instead, a large self-sealing tank was installed in the fuselage. This caused the cockpit to be moved three feet aft of its original position, the only major change made in the Corsair's basic design. Four .50-caliber machine guns were placed in the wings, and the ammunition capacity was greatly increased. Final armament, however, was six .50s in the wings. The XF4U-1 had had two nose guns—a .30 and a .50, synchronized to fire through the prop—and two .50s in the wings. The bomb receptacles on the prototype were removed, although the Corsair was later to gain considerable fame as a bomber. Additional armor plate, weighing 170 pounds, was added to the seat, deck, oil tank, and behind the pilot. Bulletproof windshield glass was installed; the arresting gear was changed; a jettisonable canopy was added. Aileron span was increased to get a higher roll rate, while a small flap in the outer wing panel was removed. An automatically released life raft was built into a few early models, but soon abandoned.

Construction-wise, changes were made to incorporate a larger number of forgings and castings to ease production bottlenecks. The tailwheel forging on the F4U-1 was the largest in use on any fighter at that time. In general, the fuselage lines were altered to accommodate the new cockpit and fuel tank location. The wing and tail area and shape were not changed and remained the same throughout the life of the

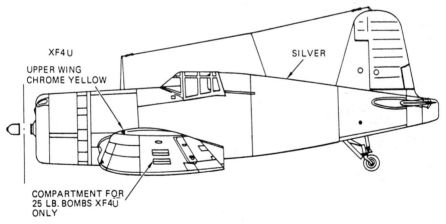

Vought XF4U-1.

aircraft with the exception of some British models, which had eight inches removed from the wings to allow clearance on British jeep carriers.

Engineering for production of the F4U-1 began December 30, 1940. A final demonstration of the XF4U-1 took place at Anacostia February 24-25, 1941, and a letter of intent was issued by the Navy on March 3, 1941. Chance Vought submitted its production proposal for the F4U-1 on April 2, 1941. Just three months later, on June 30, the Navy awarded Vought the contract to build the F4U-1. This was followed on November 1, 1941, by contracts to Brewster Aeronautical Corporation to build the Corsair (to carry the designation F3A-1). Goodyear Aircraft was named an associate contractor on the F4U-1 in December, 1941. The Goodyear model designation was FG-1.

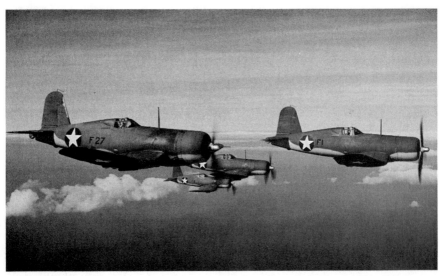

Very early production F4U-1s with framed canopy in aft position. Fuselage cutouts directly behind hood improved visibility in rear, but not enough. (U.S. Navy Photograph)

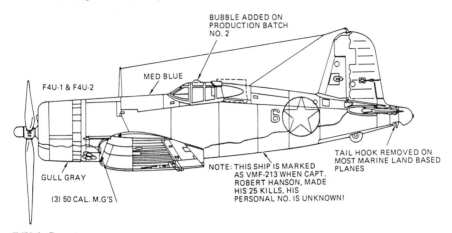

F4U-1 Corsair.

But even before issuing the production contracts, the Navy asked for a follow-on proposal on June 14, 1941, for an XF4U-3, a high-altitude fighter to be equipped with a new two-stage supercharger developed by Turbo-Engineering Company of Trenton, New Jersey. Chance Vought built only three XF4U-3s. In 1944, Goodyear converted 27 airframes to this model, although the number was later reduced to 13. Tests were conducted at the Naval Air Material Center, Philadelphia, into 1946. Results showed the superchargers capable of maintaining sea level density at more than 40,000 feet.

The first production F4U-1 (Bureau of Aeronautics No. 02153) flew June 25, 1942. It had a maximum speed of 415 miles per hour, sea level rate of climb of 3,120 feet per minute, and a service ceiling of 37,000 feet. Gross weight in combat condition was 12,060 pounds.

Meanwhile, Chance Vought had submitted a proposal on January 6, 1942, for a night fighter version, the XF4U-2. On January 28, the Navy inspected a mockup, but production pressures prevented the company from manufacturing the -2 model. The Naval Aircraft Factory at Philadelphia converted 12 standard F4U-1s to F4U-2s, equipping them with airborne intercept radar and autopilots. They eventually saw service with VF(N)-75 and VF(N)-101.

Cockpit of F4U-1. (Ling-Temco-Vought)

While production and development work was going on at the Vought plant, the Navy carried out extensive flight tests with the F4U-1 following delivery of the first production model on July 31, 1942. First carrier qualification trials were held September 25, 1942, aboard the USS *Sangamon* in Chesapeake Bay. F4U-1 number seven (BuAir No. 02159), with Commander Sam Porter at the controls, made the tests. Four landings and takeoffs were completed. Indicated airspeed on landing was 85 knots (wind over the deck was 28 knots). Takeoff distance was 280 feet. Several criticisms of the early F4U-1s resulted from carrier trials and other flight tests. Oil from the hydraulically operated cowl flaps and engine valve pushrods spattered the pilot's goggles and the windshield during landings. The problem persisted until a single master cylinder replaced a number of individual cylinders and the top section of the engine cowl permanently sealed in December 1942. The long nose, ending in a huge powerplant, made for poor visibility in the three-point touchdown attitude. This was remedied by raising the entire cockpit unit starting with the 689th Corsair produced. This raised cabin variation was designated the F4U-1A. A one-piece bubble canopy was added at the same time to the F4U-1A models. A stiff landing gear created a bounce on landing and was the primary reason for Corsairs being declared unsuitable for Navy carrier use until late in 1944. The fighter also had a landing "twitch," or directional kick on touchdown. Raising the tailwheel and adding a small spoiler to the leading edge of the right wing eliminated the problem. It was caused by local stalling of one wing just as the airplane slowed to land.

Brewster F3A-1 (F4U-1) with early framed canopy. Bomb attachments, pioneered by Brewster, are visible under the leading edge of the outer wing panels. Plagued with management troubles, Brewster completed only 735 Corsairs. (Brewster Aeronautical Corporation)

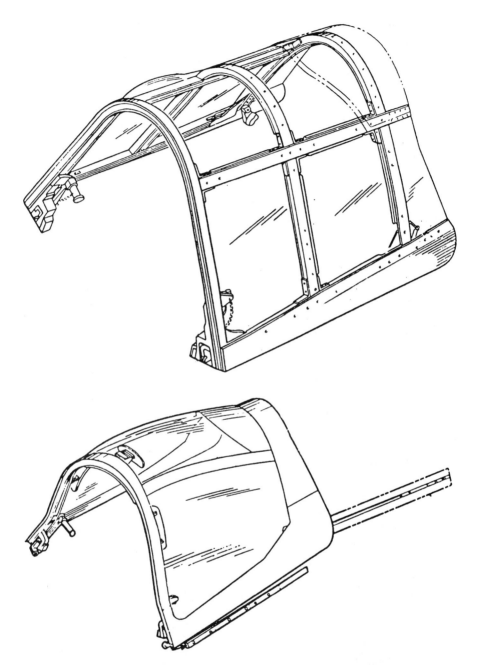

The original framed Corsair canopy (top) was relocated three feet aft in the F4U-1 design, which caused visibility problems. To remedy this problem, the cockpit was raised in the F4U-1A model and a one-piece bubble canopy replaced the framed canopy (bottom). This new canopy was used in all subsequent Corsair modifications.

As 1942 drew to a close, 178 F4U-1s had rolled off the production line at Vought's Stratford, Connecticut, plant. The first Corsairs allocated to combat units had gone to Marine Fighter Squadron 124 (VMF-124) in late September. VMF-124 was to be the first unit to take the Corsair into the fight. Navy Fighter Squadron 12 (VF-12), formed at North Island in October 1942 became the first Navy Corsair-equipped outfit.

To prepare the Corsair for combat operations, a modification center was formed at Air Base Group Two, Fleet Marine Force West Coast, in November under Colonel Stanley Ridderhoff, USMC. A total of 159 changes were made to the F4U-1 before it was declared combat-ready. After 25 days of round-the-clock work, 22 aircraft were turned over to VMF-124 on December 28, 1942, with an additional 22 ready for VF-12 by January 22, 1943. The Corsair was going to war.

During combat practice in early January 1943, a captured Japanese Zero was put up against an F4U-1, with the Corsair proving superior in most respects. Against a P-51 Mustang, the Corsair outfought the Army craft above 12,000 feet, and was considered evenly matched below that altitude. A pair of Corsairs took on two Grumman F6F Hellcats. Noted Navy flier Butch O'Hare piloted one of the Hellcats, and later flew the Corsair. Observers said the Hellcat was no match for the F4U-1. On May 21, 1943, a fighter evaluation meeting took place at Eglin Air Base in Florida. Army pilots flying the Corsair for the first time were high in their praise. Dogfights were held with P-47, P-51, P-38, and P-39 Army fighters and all resulted favorably for the Corsair.

On February 26, 1943, pilots of VF-12 held their first night flying maneuvers in Corsairs. VF-12 engaged in field carrier practice landings at North Island on March 3. Two pilots qualified aboard the carrier USS *Core* (CVE) on March 4 when Lt.

The F4U-1A with full bubble canopy was the final answer to the visibility problem. Pilot seat could be raised or lowered, giving better forward sighting for improved gunnery. The first fighter-bomber version of the Corsair, F4U-1D had twin fuselage bomb pylons. Armament was six .50-caliber machine guns. (National Archives)

Commander Clifton and Lt. (jg) John Magda made four landings each in F4U-1s (BuAir Nos. 02234 and 02307). The entire squadron qualified in April. However, the Navy did not clear the Corsair for carrier duty. In fact, when VF-12 reached the combat area later in 1943, they were ordered to turn their F4U-1s over to the Marines while they were re-equipped with F6Fs.

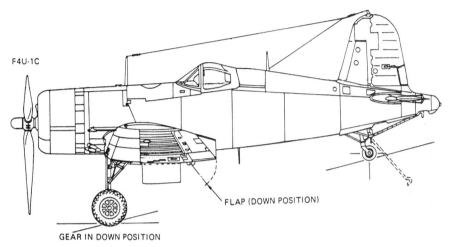

F4U-1C

FLAP (DOWN POSITION)

GEAR IN DOWN POSITION

F4U-1C Corsair.

British Royal Navy put Corsairs in full carrier service nine months before U.S. Navy. Corsair II (upper left) in landing attitude. Note squared wingtips due to removal of eight inches from each wing for hangar deck clearance of the smaller British carriers. (Ministry of Defense [Navy]

The first Corsairs destined for British service arrived in England in November 1943. By early 1944, the Royal Navy was regularly operating Corsairs from their carriers—at least nine months ahead of the U.S. Navy. Corsairs flown from carrier decks played a significant part in the crippling attack against the German battleship *Tirpitz* in Norway's Alten Fjord, April 3, 1944. British Navy Corsairs also began appearing over the Indian Ocean as well as in the Pacific Theater.

But entering the second year of combat, the Corsair was still not acceptable for Navy carrier assignment. Even the British reports on carrier suitability and the Corsair's outstanding combat record as a land-based fighter did not sway the Navy. The controversy came to a point in March 1944, when the Chief of Naval Air Operational Training, Jacksonville, drafted a letter condemning the Corsair as a carrier-based weapon. The same reasons were again cited: In the hands of inexperienced pilots, the F4U tended to bounce on landing. The student pilot attrition rate was too high. Fortunately, the letter was not transmitted, thus giving Chance Vought a final opportunity to cure the problem.

Spearheaded by Vought's tireless service manager, Jack Hospers, "Project Dog" was instituted immediately. This program, one of four presented by Vought engineers, took just ten days to put into effect. Going right to the heart of the problem, the oleo characteristics of the landing gear leg were improved, and the persistent "built-in bounce" was eliminated for good. Results of test flights with the improved gear were so successful that the Corsair received immediate endorsement.

All remaining doubts about the F4U's landing characteristics were dispelled aboard the carrier USS *Gambier Bay* in April 1944. Navy Squadron VF-301, flying F4U-1s with modified oleo struts, completed 113 landings without incident.

Goodyear Aircraft Corporation had built almost 4,000 FG-1 and FG-1D Corsairs by the summer of 1944. Goodyear FG-1D was similar to Vought F4U-1D. Armament was six machine guns, underwing rocket launchers, and twin fuselage pylons. (Goodyear Aircraft Corporation)

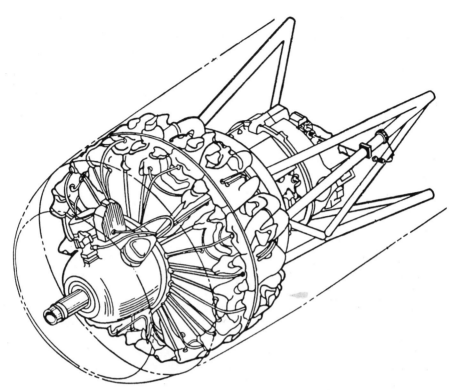

The 2,000-plus-hp Corsair engine was the largest fitted to a fighter plane to that time. Despite the engine weight and power, the steel tubing engine mount design was a model of simplicity.

Immediately the Navy ordered all Corsairs on the West Coast to be retrofitted with the new struts. At last, the F4U was completely accepted for carrier service.

While Vought and the Navy were wrestling with the carrier acceptance, work continued on further development of the Corsair. The Navy had ordered 200 equipped with four 20mm cannon instead of the six .50s. These were designated F4U-1C. An increase in power was featured when the Navy received the first models equipped with water-injection engines on November 25, 1943. By moving the throttle an additional ⅜" beyond full power setting, a brief period of water-injection operation could be employed, resulting in a boost of 250 horsepower.

On April 22, 1944, the Navy accepted the first model fitted with twin pylons for carrying bombs or droppable fuel tanks. This was the F4U-1D, the first fighter-bomber version of the Corsair. The first -1D models had bomb racks under each outer wing panel capable of carrying a 100-pound bomb. Later versions incorporated a fuselage centerline rack designed by Brewster that could carry either a 500 or 1,000-pounder. That the Corsair could always exceed its design limits was demonstrated by Charles A. Lindbergh, a tech rep for United Aircraft, when he took off in a Corsair for an attack on Wotje Atoll with a 4,000-pound bomb load!

In a number of other instances, 2,000-pound bombs were carried. With these heavy loads, the Corsair soon developed into an excellent dive bomber. The first such mission was flown in March 1944 by VMF-111, and in the following seven weeks, the Marine Corsairs dropped 200,000 pounds of bombs on the enemy.

On January 25, 1944, Chance Vought received a Navy letter of intent on a company proposal to build the XF4U-4. The first production model flew September 20, 1944, and was accepted by the Navy on October 31. Equipped with the new Pratt and Whitney R-2800-18W (water injection) engine and a four-bladed, 13 feet 2 inch-diameter Hamilton-Standard propeller, the new Corsair was rated at 451 miles per hour.

Night fighting F4U-4N carried APS-6 search radar in starboard radome. F4U-4 was first Corsair to have four-bladed prop. Chin inlet provided engine air. (U.S. Navy Photograph)

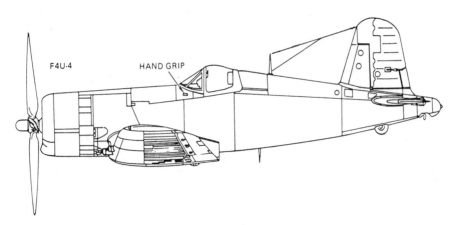

F4U-4 Corsair.

The F4U-4, with a rate of climb of 4,400 feet per minute and a service ceiling of 40,200 feet, was the Navy's answer to the much-improved Japanese interceptors arriving in the Pacific. In addition to the new powerplant, the F4U-4 featured a completely redesigned cockpit, a new canopy, an armor-plated bucket seat, and regrouped instruments. A change was also made to a downdraft-type carburetor, and intake ducts were moved from the wings to the cowl. Additional fighter-bomber ordnance was possible with the addition of rocket launchers on the outer wing panels. The gross combat weight was 12,310 pounds. An F4U-4C version had four 20mm cannon with 924 rounds per gun; 300 F4U-4Cs were ordered.

The prototype XF4U-5 flew December 21, 1944, equipped with sidewheel supercharged Pratt and Whitney engine, as a high-altitude fighter designed to operate at 45,000 feet. This Corsair did not reach production before the end of World War II. However, the war's end did not finish the Corsair. A Navy letter of intent was received February 6, 1946, on Vought's proposal to build the F4U-5 and it went into production immediately. The R-2800-32(E) engine put out approximately 200 horsepower more than the previous model, and maintained greater power to a higher critical altitude. Maximum speed was 480 miles per hour; rate of climb was upped to 5,240 feet per minute at sea level. Other features included automatic controls

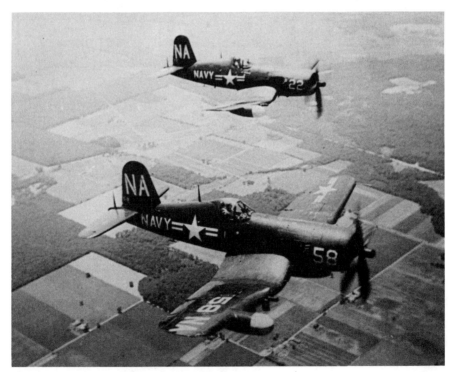

The Vought Corsair was used extensively during the Korean war in many roles. Two F4U-5NL all-weather Corsairs are shown. Special effort was made for pilot comfort in the -5NL under the most severe weather conditions. All production F4U-5s had two cheek air inlets. These supply twin superchargers. (U.S. Navy Photograph)

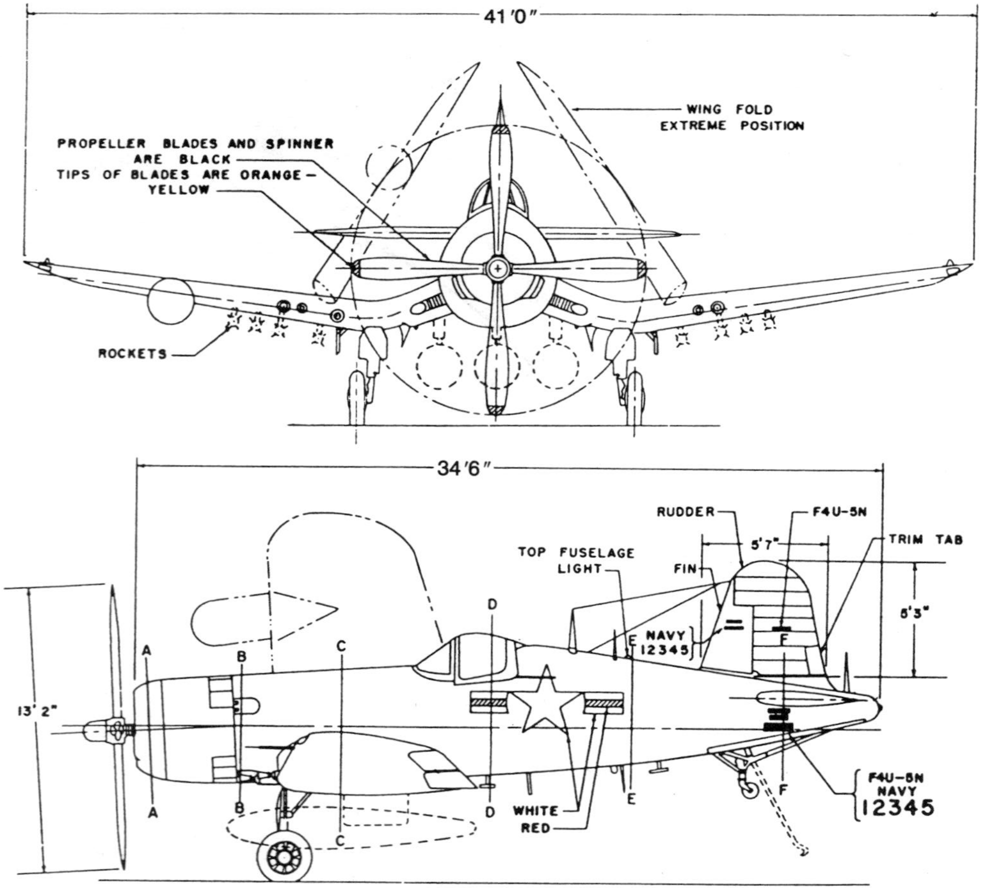

WING FOLD
EXTREME POSITION

41'0"

PROPELLER BLADES AND SPINNER
ARE BLACK
TIPS OF BLADES ARE ORANGE—
YELLOW

ROCKETS

TRIM TAB

5'3"

F4U-5N

5'7"

F4U-5N
NAVY
12345

RUDDER

FIN

E NAVY
12345

TOP FUSELAGE
LIGHT

34'6"

WHITE

RED

D

C

B

A

13'2"

F4U-5N Corsair.

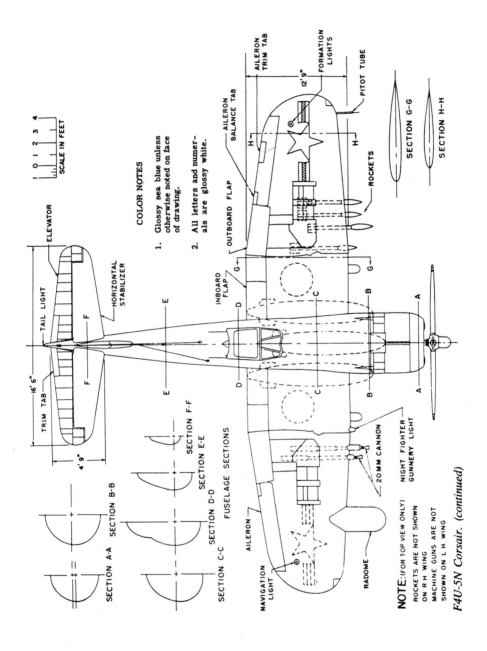

SCALE IN FEET

COLOR NOTES

1. Glossy sea blue unless otherwise noted on face of drawing.

2. All letters and numerals are glossy white.

ELEVATOR

HORIZONTAL STABILIZER

TAIL LIGHT

TRIM TAB

16' 6"

4' 9"

AILERON TRIM TAB

FORMATION LIGHTS

PITOT TUBE

AILERON BALANCE TAB

OUTBOARD FLAP

12' 9"

ROCKETS

SECTION G-G

SECTION H-H

INBOARD FLAP

SECTION B-B

SECTION A-A

SECTION D-D

SECTION C-C

FUSELAGE SECTIONS

SECTION F-F

SECTION E-E

AILERON

NAVIGATION LIGHT

RADOME

20 MM CANNON

NIGHT FIGHTER GUNNERY LIGHT

NOTE: (FOR TOP VIEW ONLY)
ROCKETS ARE NOT SHOWN ON R H WING
MACHINE GUNS ARE NOT SHOWN ON L H WING

F4U-5N Corsair. (continued)

17

for the supercharger, cowl flaps, intercooler doors and oil cooler doors. The combat power system was automated, and considerable attention was paid to pilot comfort. The redesigned cowl had air inlets at the four o'clock and eight o'clock positions. For the first time, the entire outer wing panels were entirely metal covered. Spring tabs on elevator and rudder eased stick loads; guns and pitot tubes were electrically heated. The nose was dropped two degrees to improve longitudinal stability and enhance forward vision.

Mounting interest in night and all-weather fighting capability lead to the F4U-5N equipped with search radar. Another offshoot became the F4U-5P long range photo reconnaissance version with a unique rotating camera mount.

In 1950 the last of the U.S. Navy Corsairs entered production as the AU-1. Designed as a low-altitude attack and close support weapon, the AU-1 saw extensive service in the Korean conflict. Heavily armored and equipped with a single stage supercharger, the AU remained in production for the Marines until 1952.

The final version of the Corsair was the F4U-7, built for the French Navy. Essentially the same aircraft as the F4U-4, it was powered with R-2800-18(W) and designed as high-altitude fighter. Thus the Corsair completed the cycle: from fighter, to dive-bomber, to fighter-bomber, to attack plane, and back to fighter. When the last one rolled off the line in February 1953, it marked the end of a production string of 12,571 aircraft. And it marked the end of high-performance propeller-driven fighters. The jets had come to stay. During its more than a dozen years of first line service, the Corsair had survived 981 major engineering changes and over 20,000 production alterations.

The Argentine Navy flew Vought F4U-5 Corsairs for many years. An Argentine Corsair is shown taking off from the carrier Independencia during the late 1960s. (Argentine Navy)

Final Corsair for U.S. forces was AU-1 built for Marines and used extensively in Korea. A low-altitude ground attack ship, rockets, bombs, and cannon were carried along with heavy armor. Shown just after takeoff, wheels are just starting to rotate and retract. (U.S. Marine Corps Photo)

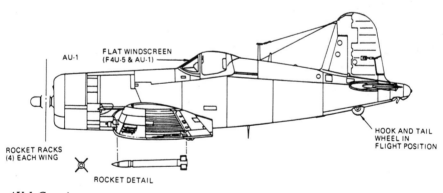

AU-1 Corsair.

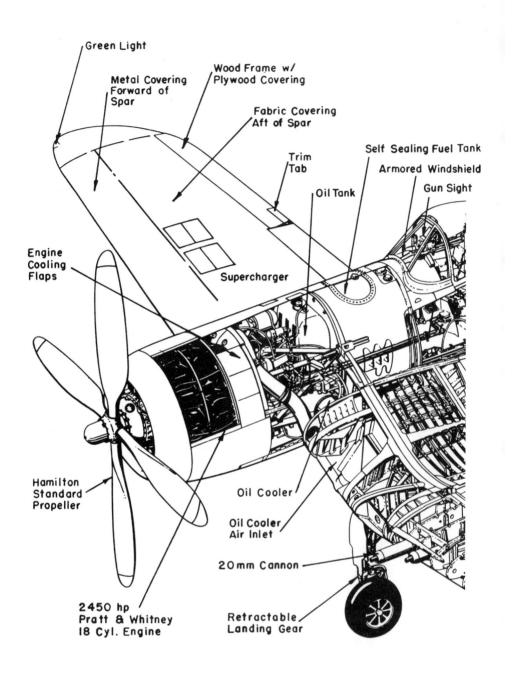

Green Light

Metal Covering Forward of Spar

Wood Frame w/ Plywood Covering

Fabric Covering Aft of Spar

Trim Tab

Oil Tank

Self Sealing Fuel Tank

Armored Windshield

Gun Sight

Engine Cooling Flaps

Supercharger

Hamilton Standard Propeller

Oil Cooler

Oil Cooler Air Inlet

20 mm Cannon

2450 hp Pratt & Whitney 18 Cyl. Engine

Retractable Landing Gear

Vought Corsair(F4U-6) AU-I

Originally designated F4U-6, change in system created AU-1, first Vought "attack" type.

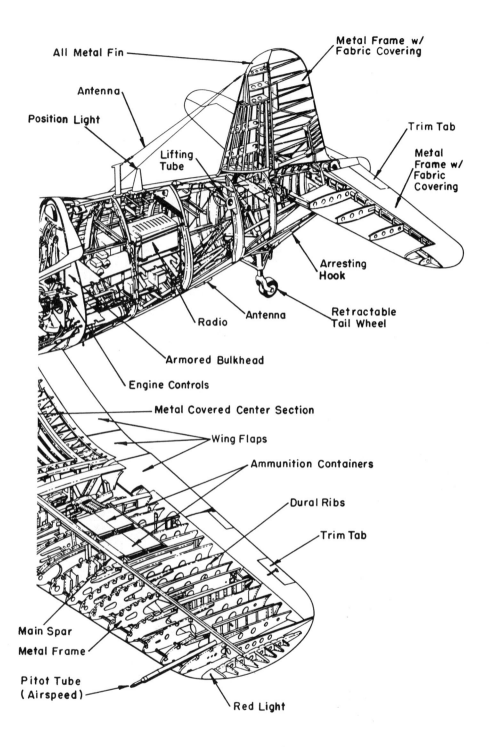

All Metal Fin

Metal Frame w/ Fabric Covering

Antenna

Position Light

Trim Tab

Lifting Tube

Metal Frame w/ Fabric Covering

Arresting Hook

Radio

Antenna

Retractable Tail Wheel

Armored Bulkhead

Engine Controls

Metal Covered Center Section

Wing Flaps

Ammunition Containers

Dural Ribs

Trim Tab

Main Spar

Metal Frame

Pitot Tube (Airspeed)

Red Light

Designed as a high-altitude fighter, the F4U-7 was quite similar to the F4U-4. Underwing rocket launchers are clearly seen. (ECP Armées [Aeronavale])

Last of the line. F4U-7 built for French, shown just after landing aboard French carrier Arromanches. (ECP Armées [Aeronavale])

Most powerful Corsair, Goodyear F2G-1D housed 3,000-hp engine, featured complete bubble canopy and low fuselage deck. Only five of the original 418 ordered were built before contract was cut; BuAir #88454 was the first, carries markings of the Naval Air Test Center. It had been developed to combat the Kamikaze menace. This design did not have folding wings. (U.S. Navy Photograph)

2

The Battleground
Through the Solomons To Victory

The bloody battle of Guadalcanal Island ended victoriously for the Allied armies early in 1943. This foothold in the southern end of the Solomon Islands opened a new phase for the United States forces in the South Pacific Theatre of Operations. Admiral Chester Nimitz and General Douglas MacArthur were now ready to take the offensive in the war against Japan.

The master plan was to have MacArthur's land forces advance westward along the coast of New Guinea to the Philippine Islands, while the naval effort under Nimitz would be directed toward the powerful Japanese stronghold on the Central Pacific island of Truk in the Caroline Island chain. The principal enemy bastion standing in the way of this strategy was the Japanese base of Rabaul on the northeastern tip of the Island of New Britain in the Bismarck Archipelago.

Rabaul controlled the path from New Guinea and Guadalcanal to the Philippines. It also served as a barrier for attacks on Truk from the south. Located as it was—700 miles south of Truk, 560 miles northwest of Guadalcanal, and only 445 miles northeast of Port Moresby on the southern coast of New Guinea—Rabaul was in the perfect defensive position to prevent the proposed Allied advance. Offensively, it was from Rabaul that the Japanese planned to dominate the Solomons, New Guinea, and the coast of Australia. As a result, with both belligerents keenly aware of the strategic importance of Rabaul, the stage was set for a long battle in which airpower was to play the decisive role.

Lost to Australia by Germany during the First World War, Rabaul was taken from the Australians during the Japanese advance in January 1942. Rabaul was blessed with one of the finest harbors in the South Pacific, protected by six volcanic mountains, and the Japanese lost no time in making it an impregnable fortress. After the fall of Guadalcanal, the importance of Rabaul increased tremendously and the strength of the bastion was built up even more until, by November 1943, there were 98,000 Japanese on New Britain. Almost 400 aircraft were based on Rabaul's four principal airfields at Lakunai, Vunakanau, Rapopo, and Tobero to bomb Allied ships and bases as well as to defend the base against the impending Allied attack. It was quite evident that the Japanese were prepared to hold Rabaul at any cost.

The logical path from Guadalcanal to Rabaul is through the Solomon Islands,

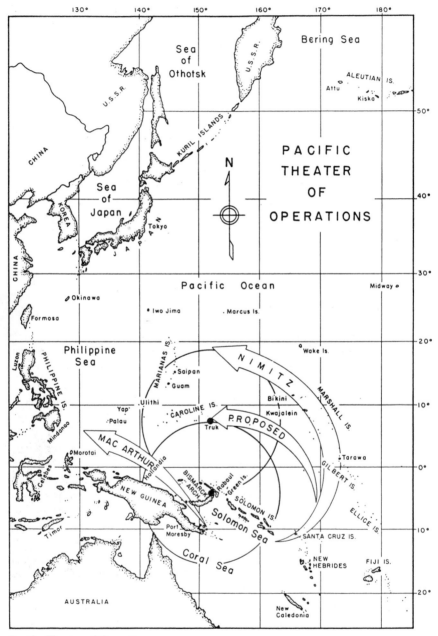

Pacific Theater of Operations.

which run in a northwest-southeast direction. This island chain is about 550 miles long, with Guadalcanal the largest of the southeastern islands and Bougainville the largest at the northwestern end. The islands roughly form two rows with a water passage between them. This is the "Slot" and became the scene of considerable naval and aerial activity.

Located between 5 and 10 degrees below the equator, the Solomons are covered with volcanic peaks and impenetrable jungles, making travel alone a hazardous task. Yet this terrain was, through necessity, the site of one of the most important of the Pacific battles.

Initially, the Americans had planned to use aircraft carriers to pound Rabaul, but by January 1943, there was not a single serviceable United States carrier in the entire Pacific! During August 1942, the *Enterprise* was severely damaged in the Battle of the Eastern Solomons. A few weeks later, Japanese torpedoes sank the *Wasp* and severely damaged the *Saratoga*. Later in 1942, during the Battle of the Santa Cruz Islands, the *Hornet* was sunk and the *Enterprise* again severely damaged.

This situation forced Nimitz to resort to an island-hopping strategy, using land-based aircraft, in order to reach Rabaul. It was fortunate that the closeness of the islands permitted the use of land-based fighters. The Japanese realized this and feverishly built airfields in the Central Solomons as they abandoned Guadalcanal.

Typical of the primitive airstrips in the South Pacific is this one on Emirau, 76 miles northwest of Japanese-held New Ireland. Crushed coral was often used for paving. This finished runway, taxiways, and revetments were hacked out of the jungle and completed in less than 60 days by Navy Seabees. (Defense Dept. Photo [Marine Corps])

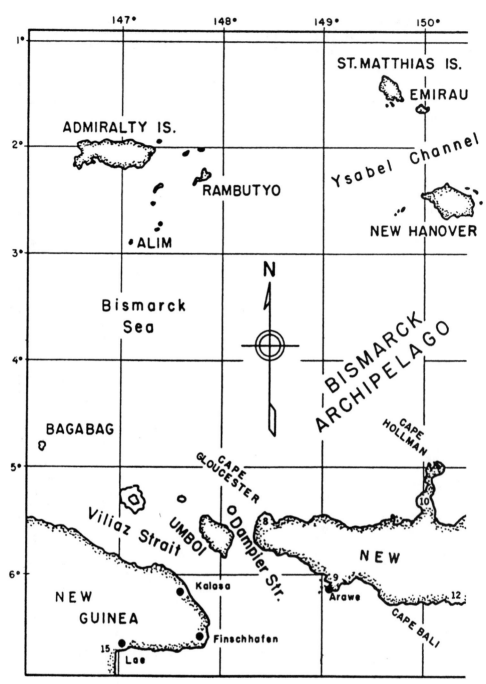

Bismarck Archipelago.

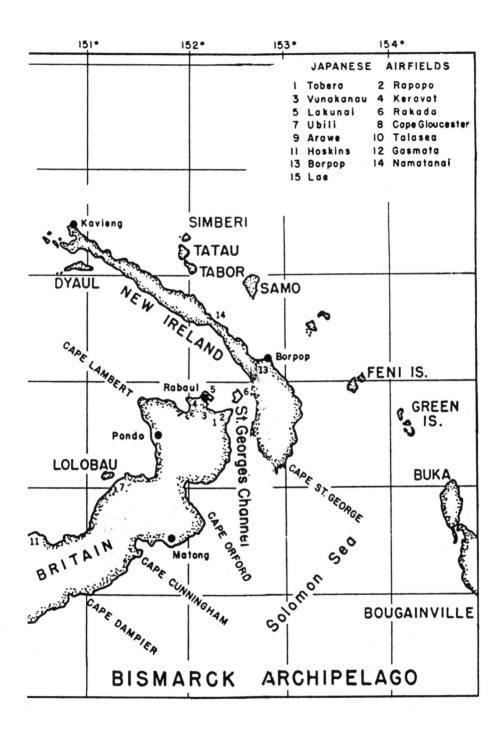

The situation now made Bougainville the basic Allied objective in the Solomons campaign. This was the largest of the chain, with the highest mountains and the wildest jungles. The sole purpose of the island-hopping strategy was to secure airfields from which short-range fighter planes could operate. The Solomon Islands now took the place of a fleet of aircraft carriers and became stepping stones to Bougainville, which would be used as the final springboard to raid Rabaul only 200 miles away. Bougainville, named after Louis Antoine de Bougainville, an 18th century navigator who was the first Frenchman to circumnavigate the Earth, boasted six airfields: Torokina, Kieta, Tenekow, Bonis, Kara, and Kahili, the largest. This was the prize the Allies coveted as they began the Solomon offensive early in 1943.

Admiral William F. "Bull" Halsey was in charge of this important operation until June 1944, and the principal force under his overall command was a conglomeration of aircraft types flown by members of the United States Navy, United States Army, United States Marine Corps, and the Royal New Zealand Air Force. Lockheed P-38 Lightnings, Bell P-39 Aircobras, Curtiss P-40 Warhawks, and Vought F4U Corsairs escorted Consolidated B-24 Liberators, North American B-25 Mitchells, Grumman TBF Avengers, and Douglas SBD Dauntless bombers to destroy Japanese airfields, supply depots, and naval craft. In few other air actions have fighter aircraft ever meant so much. In addition to escort, ground strafing and interception duties, enormous fighter sweeps were the order of the day to flush out the enemy fighter force and destroy it.

The Army Air Corps provided all the heavy bombers and about 20 percent of the fighters while the RNZAF and the United States Navy supplied a token force of land-based fighters and PB4Y heavy bombers. In view of the fact that this was a land-based action, well suited to the Marines, and that they already had a toehold in the Solomons fighting thanks to the "cactus air force" with their Grumman F4F Wildcats, Marine Aviation became the principal air arm during this campaign. It was here that it made its greatest contribution toward winning the war and many of the Marine fighter pilots blossomed into America's finest aces.

When the first Corsairs arrived on Guadalcanal in early 1943, the Japanese were still having things pretty much their own way. The excellent Zero was more than a match for the Grumman F4F Wildcat, then the best Marine fighter in combat. On their first mission, 12 F4Us of VMF-124 escorted Navy PB4Ys to Bougainville, a 300-mile hop that had been out of the question for the short-range Wildcat. During this flight, a Japanese Zero pilot came down and looked over the "bent-wing birds" with undisguised curiosity. Although he didn't know it, he was looking at the first American fighter that could outperform his own.

On the third day in the combat area, February 14, the inexperienced pilots of VMF-124 got their first taste of Japanese skill and aggressiveness in the Solomons. Fifty Zeroes jumped the Navy bombers and their escorts with such devastating results that the battle became known as the "St. Valentine's Day Massacre." Only two F4Us were lost, but the Japanese destroyed an additional eight Allied craft.

Although the Marines' first experiences were not as hoped for, the Corsairs soon proved themselves the masters of the best Japan had to offer. Within six months, all Marine squadrons in the South Pacific were Corsair-equipped. As the fighting

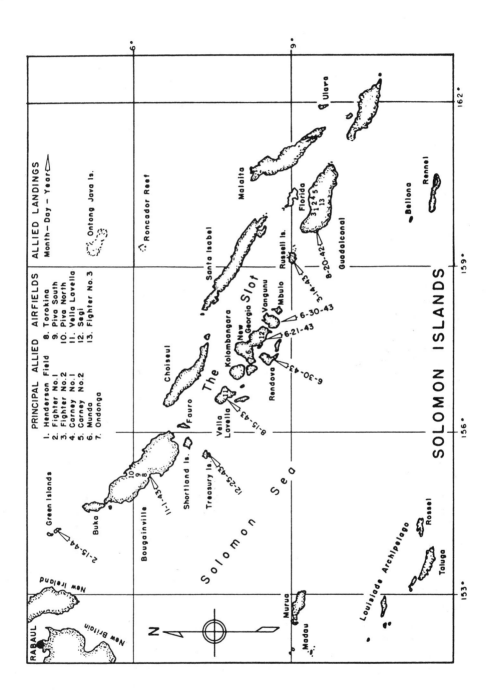

PRINCIPAL ALLIED AIRFIELDS

1. Henderson Field
2. Fighter No. 1
3. Fighter No. 2
4. Carney No. 1
5. Carney No. 2
6. Munda
7. Ondonga
8. Torokina
9. Piva South
10. Piva North
11. Vella Lavella
12. Sagi
13. Fighter No. 3

ALLIED LANDINGS

Month – Day – Year

SOLOMON ISLANDS

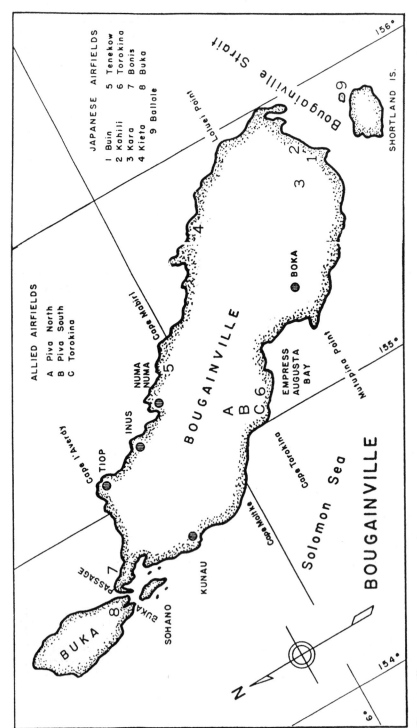

Bougainville.

moved up the Solomons chain, the airplane the enemy dubbed "The Whistling Death" lead the way. The Japanese nickname came from the peculiar whistle emitted by the air howling through the intakes located in the wing roots of the Corsair.

The American forces made the first move with a lightning thrust to Banika Island in the Russell Islands. The landing on February 21 was unopposed by the Japanese, and three weeks later Marine Air Group 21 was operating from a new airfield. Imperial Japanese Headquarters realized that the United States airpower in the Solomons must be crushed in order to relieve the threat against Rabaul and therefore organized a series of air attacks against Guadalcanal and Banika.

Admiral Isoroku Yamamoto himself went to Rabaul to personally direct the action and ordered about 100 fighters and 70 dive bombers and torpedo planes off the aircraft carriers *Zuikaku*, *Junyo*, *Hiyo*, and *Zuiho* to join 86 fighters, 27 dive bombers, and 72 twin-engine bombers and torpedo planes on Rabaul. This activity was known as "I Operation" and began on April 1 when 58 Zeroes and dive bombers swept down on the "Slot" in an effort to knock out the growing American fighter strength in the southern Solomons.

The Americans met the challenge and 18 Japanese fell before the guns of the Navy and Marine defenders. The United States forces lost 10 aircraft. On April 7 the determined Japanese sent 67 Val dive bombers and 110 Zeroes to raid the shipping that was assembled at Guadalcanal and Florida Island. Seventy-six fighters rose to stop this armada including VMF (Marine fighting squadron) 213, 214, and 221. The United States pilots lost seven aircraft while they destroyed 12 dive bombers and 27 fighters.

Torokina airfield on Bougainville had only one airstrip, but it was an important base from which to attack Rabaul. (Defense Dept. Photo [Marine Corps])

After two more similar fiascoes, Yamamoto returned the remaining carrier planes to their ships. On the 25th day of the month, four Vought Corsairs inadvertently ran into a fleet of 16 Japanese bombers escorted by about 25 Zeroes. Despite the overwhelming odds, the Marines of VMF-213 destroyed five Zeroes and lost only two aircraft!

To bolster the dwindling air fleet on New Britain and Bougainville, Admiral Mineichi Koga, who succeeded Yamamoto, sent 58 fighters and 49 twin-engine bombers from Truk to Rabaul on May 10, 1943. Three days later, Army and Marine fliers intercepted a force of 25 Zeroes escorting a reconnaissance plane headed for Guadalcanal. Again the Japanese suffered the greater losses when 15 Zeroes fell before the Marine F4U guns and another was shot down by an Army P-38 Lightning. The Americans lost only three Corsairs.

On June 7, the story was the same when Koga sent 112 Japanese pilots down the "Slot" into the jaws of the Allied fighters. U.S. Army, Navy, and Marine and New Zealand fighter planes scored heavily in a big dogfight near the Russell Islands and destroyed 23 Japanese planes while four Corsairs and one Curtiss P-40 were lost. Nine days later, 120 Japanese roared down from Rabaul and Bougainville. VMF-121, 122, and 124 helped Army and Navy pilots and antiaircraft fire destroy no less than 107 of the raiders while the United States losses amounted to only six aircraft!

Following the island-hopping timetable up the Solomons to secure more advanced air bases, United States landings were started on Munda in New Georgia on June 21, 1943. Nine days later, twin landings occurred on Vangunu and Rendova. Unlike the Banika landings in February, the enemy forces now resisted the landings with great ferocity and sent countless dive bombers and torpedo planes out in force in an attempt to destroy the invasion fleets. The Allied forces documented a total of 101 kills over the beaches of Rendova and Vangunu on June 30. Four Marine Corsair

Rabaul's Simpson Harbor was provided with natural protection by a ring of volcanic peaks. The photograph was taken during a bombing raid against Japanese shipping. White rings and disks on water surface are bomb explosions. (U.S. Air Force)

squadrons destroyed over half of the total as follows: VMF-121 (18), VMF-122 (4), VMF-213 (20), VMF-221 (16). Allied losses were only 14 aircraft and seven pilots.

The fighter planes bore the responsibility for the success or failure of the landings throughout the Solomon Islands, and in order to protect the beaches and shipping from the Japanese air fleets, they were called upon to continuously patrol the area and fight the finest pilots in Japan. The Vought F4U Corsairs flown by Marine pilots took the lion's share of the victories during this campaign. Typical of the heroic action was the raid on July 7, when 12 twin-engine Japanese Betty bombers escorted by 60 Zeroes attacked the Allied shipping off Rendova with the result that the bombers never reached their objective, thanks to the outstanding Allied fighter pilots.

Due to the effectiveness of the United States fighter force, Japanese airpower in the Solomons was gradually losing its offensive punch. This, plus the fact that several Allied fighter bases were now ready in the central Solomons, signaled the beginning of heavy bomber air strikes against the principal Solomons objective— Bougainville, springboard to Rabaul. Almost daily the heavy Army bombers struck at Kahili with their mixed fighter escort during July, August, and September. Munda fell on August 5 and nine days later VMF-123 and VMF-124 were operating from this new base.

The United States forces skipped Kolombangara and its 10,000 Japanese and landed on Vella Lavella on August 15, 1943. The bypassed Japanese evacuated Kolombangara for Rabaul during September and October as the United States bombing raids against Torokina in Empress Augusta Bay on Bougainville increased in intensity to an unbelievable crescendo. The Japanese defenders suffered such staggering losses that Admiral Koga ordered 173 more planes off his aircraft carriers,

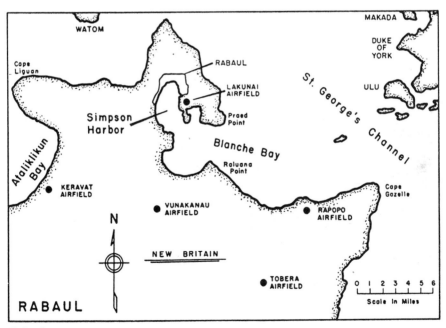

Rabaul.

on October 28, to bolster the decimated forces at Rabaul. The bombings continued, with the heavies based on New Guinea and the short-range escort fighters flying from airstrips carved out of the steaming jungles or on the sandy beaches of New Georgia and Vella Lavella.

At last the time was ripe for the long awaited Bougainville invasion. "Love Day," code name for the operation, was on November 1, 1943. The Japanese sent 120 aircraft from Rabaul to stop the Allied forces on the beaches of Empress Augusta Bay and lost 22 of their finest pilots in the futile attempt. The following day saw 89 Zeroes and 18 dive bombers strike at United States naval craft near Bougainville, but the loss of 25 more aircraft forced the attackers to retire before effective bomb hits could be made.

The next few weeks witnessed many enormous air battles over Bougainville as both sides fought stubbornly for the "springboard." When the Japanese diverted part of their Central Pacific Fleet to the Rabaul area, the United States Navy countered this move by sending the aircraft carriers *Essex*, *Independence*, and *Bunker Hill* to

The primitive conditions on the jungle airfields made maintenance and repair very difficult for the mechanics. Repair crews of VMF-211 repair battle damage on the wing guns and fuselage fuel cell of an F4U-1A on Bougainville. The importance of these men cannot be over-emphasized because they kept the battered fighter planes in flying condition and thereby enabled the Navy and Marine pilots to continue their assault on the Japanese-held islands. Mechanic is standing in access opening of massive main fuel cell forward of cockpit. (U.S. Marine Corps Photo)

join the *Saratoga* and *Princeton*, which were already in the Solomons battle area. The Marine squadrons were actively engaged in ground support work and maintaining air cover over the beaches.

By the middle of November the beach was secure. The only objective on Bougainville was a landing field for the short-range fighters and dive bombers and therefore a semicircle was carved out of the jungles at Cape Torokina on Empress Augusta Bay. The invading troops held the 40,000 Japanese soldiers at bay along the beachhead perimeter, which was roughly six by eight miles in size, while three

Portable grease rack (right) in use on landing gear. Wind howling through oil coolers in wing roots gave Corsair Japanese nickname "Whistling Death."

airfields were hastily made ready for operation. The aircraft were forced to fly from these fields within earshot of the prolonged fighting as the United States troops guarded the perimeter. The three air strips were Piva North, Piva South, and Torokina itself.

The air raids on Rabaul increased in addition to attacks on the other Bougainville airfields, especially Kahili. The raids were of two types: conventional two- and four-engine bomber strikes with fighter escorts, and enormous fighter sweeps aimed at reducing the Japanese fighter forces to impotence. In addition, many enemy installations on Rabaul were strafed by the fighters based on Bougainville. One of the Rabaul raids took place on Christmas Day 1943, with 15 bombers and 63 escort fighters shooting down 13 of the defending fighters. Raids continued through January, and between December 17, 1943, and January 1, 1944, the fighter sweeps destroyed 147 Japanese planes in the air.

On January 9, 1944, dive bombers and torpedo planes began to operate from the Piva airfields and attacked Japanese shipping around Rabaul in an effort to sever supply lines to the bastion. These dive bombing and torpedo attacks were so successful that after January the larger Japanese ships did not venture near the waters around Rabaul. The escorting Corsairs also exacted a terrific toll from the defending fighter planes. Japanese air losses were so severe that Admiral Koga transferred 98 more aircraft from Truk to Rabaul during the last days of January to build up Rabaul's airpower to 300 planes.

Royal New Zealand Air Force operated Corsairs from 1943 on. Most were Corsair II types (F4U-1D) shown in rare photo of large formation in Solomons. RNZAF often teamed with Navy and Marine units to provide escort cover in Solomons. (Royal New Zealand Air Force)

During January and February 1944, the United States Marines flew over 2,000 sorties against Rabaul while the United States Army flew 1,200. Total sorties against Rabaul during the period between November 1942 and August 1945 were: United States Marine Aviation, 14,718; United States Army Air Corps, 7,490; United States Navy, 4,608; British Empire (mainly RNZAF), 2,538. It is evident that the burden of aerial activity in the Solomons campaign fell upon the U.S. Marine Corps. And, in turn, the Marine Squadrons depended heavily upon the Vought F4U Corsair, which made its combat debut in the fighting.

As the Navy and Marine pilots steadily reduced Japanese fighter strength, the incidence of air-to-air combat rapidly fell off. Thus the Corsair had to accept ground targets, and in so doing, became one of the most effective attack and dive bombers ever built. Throughout the Solomons, Gilberts, and Marshalls campaigns, Corsairs developed into devastating strategic and ground support weapons—a combination not normally possible, but handled superbly by the versatile Vought.

Corsair 122, an F4U-1D assigned to VMF-111, was the only aircraft to receive a citation. A plaque affixed to her instrument panel states:

In accomplishing her 100 missions, Corsair 122 logged more than 400 hours flying time; her total hops, including tests and reconnaissance flights, reached an amazing total of 178. Built for air combat, Corsair 122 proved her versatility by accepting 1,000 pound bombs slung from her belly, and without strain or protest developed into the hottest dive bomber with wings. Were there blood in her fuel line instead of 100 octane, she would be wearing the Purple Heart; for the patch on the leading edge of her wing *attests to the accuracy of Jap antiaircraft fire. She has covered all the Jap bases in the Marshall Islands like the morning dew.

Corsair II of RNZAF No. 18 Squadron. (Royal New Zealand Air Force)

The constant pounding of Rabaul's airfields and shipping by the Allied fliers enabled General MacArthur to land a few troops at Arawe on the southern coast of New Britain by December 15, 1943, and at Cape Gloucester on the western tip of the island 11 days later. This invasion diverted some of the aircraft from Rabaul. However, these were soon forced to return to protect the all-important stronghold. The long Allied air campaign achieved such impressive results that, in the final analysis, the Allied command decided that an invasion of Rabaul was not necessary after all!

With all shipping cut off from Rabaul and her air fleet reduced to impotence, the once-powerful air and naval base no longer posed a threat to the advancing Allied forces. It was therefore decided to bypass Rabaul early in 1944. The Green Islands, 115 miles east of Rabaul, were the first to be invaded in a new bypass strategy when New Zealand troops covered by eight Marine squadrons landed on February 15. The Admiralty Islands, 375 miles northwest of the Japanese base, were invaded during the following month while the island of Emirau, only 90 miles north of Rabaul, felt the impact of an Allied landing on March 20, 1944. Despite the fact that Rabaul was no longer a threat it was now necessary to maintain the base in a state of constant impotence. As a result, the U.S. Marines still bombed it throughout the summer of 1944 from airfields on the Green Islands and Emirau while the giant Army bombers prepared for the assault on Truk from the same bases.

"Ole 122" of VMF-111, "Devil Dogs," was the only warplane to receive an official citation. This F4U-1D made 100 fighter-bomber sweeps without mechanical trouble during a six-month period. (U.S. Marine Corps Photo)

About 21,000 tons of bombs rained on Rabaul during the siege. After the middle of February only token Japanese air resistance was met by Marine fliers. On February 20 the Japanese evacuated as many aircraft as they could to Truk, a definite sign that the 90,000 troops in the Bismarck Archipelago were being abandoned to defend themselves as best they could. Rabaul's last contact with the homeland was during April of 1944 when a Japanese cargo submarine entered Simpson Harbor undetected by the Allied blockade.

Marine mechanic Staff Sergeant W. Howard Miller paints another bomb on the fuselage of "Ole 122" while line chief Master Technical Sergeant Fred Smith watches. (U.S. Marine Corps Photo)

It was indeed fortunate that an invasion of Rabaul was not necessary because the loss of Allied soldiers during such a frontal assault would have been enormous. The bloodshed at Tarawa, Iwo Jima, and Okinawa might have been overshadowed when compared to the attempt on this fortress. Despite the fact that her air power had been decimated and her supply route severed, Rabaul was well prepared to combat an invasion of any magnitude. All beaches were fortified with underwater mines, concrete anti-boat blocks, land mines, pillboxes, barbed wire, and plenty of ammunition! Three hundred and fifty miles of underground caves and tunnels afforded the Japanese excellent shelter from the shower of Allied bombs. In fact, it took about four tons of bombs to kill one Japanese soldier during the entire campaign! Rabaul's radar afforded them from one half hour to a full hour advance warning of an air attack, which made surprise raids by the Allies an impossibility.

In addition to an abundance of ammunition, Rabaul had plenty of food supplemented with extensive vegetable gardens. Even items such as toothpaste and soap were in plentiful supply. Morale on Rabaul was always high. Yes, it can definitely be said that the victory of the Corsair fighter pilots in the skies over the Solomons and Bismarcks was the principal factor in canceling the Rabaul invasion, thereby saving the lives of countless thousands of Allied infantrymen.

A Navy Corsair fires eight deadly five-inch rockets. Top: First rockets streak from the Corsair. Middle: Hard on the first pair of rockets, another pair appears. Bottom: Six rockets are in flight as the seventh and eighth are fired. Rockets were first used by Corsairs against ground targets on the Japanese mainland in early 1945. At that time, only four five-inch rockets were carried. (U.S. Navy Photograph)

Even more important than the cancellation of the Rabaul invasion itself was the fact that the Solomons air battles sapped the strength of the Imperial Japanese Naval Air Service. Realizing the importance of Rabaul, the Japanese fought tenaciously to hold the fortress against the Allied fighters. However, Admiral Koga underestimated the ability of the U.S. Marine and Navy pilots and their Corsairs; committing his fighter strength piecemeal, he hoped that each succeeding air battle would end the threat to Rabaul. The Admiral can be compared to a gambler at the gaming tables who enters a losing streak. In order to recoup his losses he borrows on his life's savings and bets it a little at a time, hoping to strike a winning number only to find himself broke with no hope of ever regaining solvency.

When the Solomons air battles were but an echo, Japan's finest combat pilots were dead. Like the gambler, Koga overextended his airpower and committed more aircraft to the defense of Rabaul than Japan could afford. In fact, Koga never planned to risk as many aircraft as he actually placed in combat. Their best pilots gone, the Japanese could not produce airmen with the degree of training that was sufficient to meet the demand of actual air-to-air combat. This lack of skilled pilots became evident during the invasion of Saipan in the Marianas Islands when on June 19, 1944, the U.S. Navy fliers destroyed no less than 383 Japanese aircraft on that single day! This is known as the "Marianas Turkey Shoot" thanks to the earlier fighter victories at Rabaul.

The Japanese fliers defending Rabaul and the Solomons fought with great skill and determination; they were the finest pilots in the Imperial Navy. Yet they were no match for the Corsair pilots who were so thorough in their job from that time to the end of the war that the Japanese air arm would be an ineffective weapon and

F4U-1D Corsairs carry 1,000-pound bombs for a raid on the Marshall Islands. (U.S. Marine Corps Photo)

the Japanese Combined Fleet would be without air support during crucial battles in the Central Pacific.

As soon as it was apparent that the advance up the Solomons was effective and that Rabaul could no longer seriously interfere with the Allied advance, MacArthur and Nimitz went into action. The General's American, Australian, and New Zealand troops began their march northwestward along the coast of New Guinea and captured the important Japanese base of Lae on September 16, 1944. Finchhafen fell two weeks later and the troops were well on their way to the Philippines. Nimitz began his drive against the Japanese on Truk. However, here again, it was decided to by-pass this Japanese base, which could no longer depend upon Rabaul for assistance. Truk was isolated from Japan by the Allied drives into the Gilbert, Marshall, Caroline and Marianas Islands. Japanese aerial resistance during these campaigns was quite meager, thanks to the effectiveness of the Solomons airmen. Thus, the superb performance of the Marine pilots in their Corsairs had far-reaching results, and contributed in great measure to the ultimate victory.

Night fighting operations began in the summer of 1944. VF(N)-75 went to work on Munda and put an end to the nocturnal activities of "Washing Machine Charlie" and other night hecklers. VF(N)-101 was operating from carriers.

A Corsair has just dropped napalm onto a Japanese bunker in the Palau Islands. Notice that the pilot has his landing gear lowered and flaps are down to slow the plane in order to plant the napalm with precision. (U.S. Marine Corps Photo)

As 1944 closed out, Corsairs in increasing numbers were going aboard the carriers. The Japanese Kamikaze attacks had severely disrupted Navy plans, and the need for massive fighter protection for the carrier task groups brought Marine squadrons on board to supplement Navy fighters. Marine VMF-124, the first unit to take the Corsair into combat, was the first assigned to carrier duty when they landed on the fast carrier USS *Essex*, December 28, 1944. Followed by other units in short order, the Corsair soon became the leading carrier-based fighter.

With the tempo of the Pacific war increasing steadily, both Navy and Marine F4Us opened 1945 with a pounding attack on Okinawa, January 3. They followed this with a massive assault on Saigon, January 12, and could take a good measure of the credit for the day's tally: 14 warships and 33 merchant vessels sunk.

In preparation for the Iwo Jima landings, Corsairs hit Tokyo on heavy fighter sweeps several times during February. The Iwo landings were closely supported by Marine fliers in rocket-firing F4Us. Concurrently, Okinawa and the Japanese home islands continued to receive heavy attention. On April 3, 16 Corsairs and an equal number of Navy Hellcats hit airbases in Japan. They ran into a flock of Zeroes bent on ramming the Corsairs. The Marines shot down 11, and the Navy got the rest.

Okinawa was invaded April 1, 1945. The F4U pilots were kept busy fending off the fierce Kamikaze attacks, but as they diminished, the Corsairs returned to ground support with increasing deliveries of rockets, bombs, and napalm. The actions throughout the campaign earned the Corsair yet another name: "The Sweetheart of Okinawa." Part of the effectiveness of the Corsair against the well dug-in enemy was the use of napalm for the first time on April 18. From that time until Okinawa was secure, the Marine fliers dropped 152,000 gallons of liquid fire across the island. Okinawa was also the scene of the first cannon-bearing Corsair attacks.

Although primarily engaged in low-altitude fighting, Corsairs continued to protect the fleet against the final efforts of Japanese pilots, Kamikaze and otherwise. In one incident, First Lieutenant Robert Klingman chased a Japanese photo plane more than 150 miles at 38,000 feet. When he drew close enough to open fire, he found his guns frozen, but bored in and rammed his quarry with the Corsair's big prop. With part of his prop missing, and pieces of the shorn off enemy's tail embedded in the wing, Klingman brought his bent-up bird back safely to Okinawa. In his first aerial combat, Second Lieutenant William Eldridge shot down four Japanese planes in four minutes! And the Marines' "Death Rattler" squadron shot down 124½ enemy planes in a whirlwind tour of duty on Okinawa without losing one of their own.

As the Navy's efforts turned to the Japanese mainland, Corsairs flew constant sorties over the airfields, factories, and transportation centers. But the planned invasion never took place. When the surrender came, nearly every carrier was equipped with the Corsair.

From the first combat engagement at Guadalcanal on February 14, 1943, through the end of World War II and on into Korea, the Corsair was an outstanding fighter. When V-J day marked the close of the war against Japan, Corsairs had carried out a total of 64,051 action sorties—54,470 from land bases, 9,581 from carrier decks.

Marine pilots led the onslaught. Operating from crude island airstrips, they shot down 1,400 enemy planes—1,100 fighters and 300 bombers. Marine air losses were

Lieut. Robert R. Klingman is a perfect example of the Corsair pilots' eagerness to get at the enemy and destroy him. He climbed to 38,000 feet to reach a Japanese Nick which was on a photographic mission, but his guns had frozen. The intrepid pilot closed in on the Japanese plane and chewed off its tail with his Corsair's 13-foot propeller! The Nick went into a violent spin and shed its wings. Kingman made a dead-stick landing with large pieces missing from his prop. (Defense Dept. Photo [Marine Corps])

but 141. A smaller number of Navy Corsairs accounted for 162 enemy aircraft with a loss of only 14 of their own, bringing the final tally to 1,560 enemy kills by land-based F4Us. After assignment to aircraft carriers, Corsairs accounted for another 578 for only 34 Corsairs lost in air combat. Claiming 2,140 enemy aircraft destroyed in the air against the loss of only 189, the Corsair entered the thick of battle to emerge with a victory ratio of 11.3 to 1.

Despite the exceptional qualities of the F4U design and its record in action, the final effectiveness of any aircraft is dependent upon the ability of the man in the cockpit. It is true that a pilot of skill and daring is handicapped by an inferior airplane. Conversely, a superior fighter plane design is all but useless without an aggressive and bold hand at the controls, the Corsair aces you are about to meet.

3

The Men
Corsair Aces Make History

Sixty-four percent of all United States Marine aerial victories during the Second World War were gained in the Solomon Islands—Rabaul area of operations. The twelve principal Marine fighter squadrons in the area all flew Corsairs, but due to the prescribed rotation policy only four to six squadrons were in action at any given time. It was customary for a unit to remain in a forward combat zone for a period of from four to six weeks, after which it was given one week leave and transported to Sydney, Australia, or Aukland, New Zealand, for a mad holiday. This was followed by two to four weeks in a back area on a relatively quiet island such as Espiritu Santo or Efate in the New Hebrides for regrouping and additional training, if required. The unit then returned to action on Guadalcanal, New Georgia, Vella Lavella, or Bougainville.

On many occasions, only a select few left the squadron and were replaced by fresh pilots. On other occasions, entire units were dissolved for leave and places were taken by new men. The old squadron name and number remained the same, however, during this turnover.

The men who became the high scorers all flew against great odds. In addition to being pitted against the finest fliers in Japan, they were forced to live under unbelievable conditions. Soaring temperatures, fantastic humidity, and torrential rains were bad enough, but on many occasions, powdered eggs, dried beef, and weevil-ridden bread were the finer delicacies adding to living pleasure during these difficult days. Engines were balky in the heat and it was not uncommon for a pilot to be forced to return to his base due to low oil pressure or overheated engine.

As soon as he left his formation, an Allied pilot would invariably be jumped by a Zero, for the Japanese fighters were on the constant prowl for stragglers. A lone American could expect to find a Zero waiting for him as far south as New Georgia, and as a result, none of the sky over the islands was considered safe territory. This required a constant vigil by the Solomons pilots during every flying moment.

Furthermore, Japanese snipers often crept close to the jungle airstrip and fired at the aircraft and pilots as they prepared to take off. With this combination of adverse conditions, it is indeed surprising that the men had any will left with which to carry on the fight.

The Marine fighter squadrons that experienced the major portion of the action in the Solomon Islands and Rabaul were VMF-122, 124, 211, 212, 213, 214, 215, and 221. These eight outstanding units are officially credited with the destruction of 903 Japanese aircraft. Of the token force of U.S. Navy aircraft that participated in the campaign, VF-17 is unquestionably the most famous, with 156 Solomons victories to its credit. The eight Solomons campaign aces selected for this volume destroyed a total of 166 ½ Japanese aircraft. They are among the finest fighters the United States forces produced during the Second World War.

Kenneth A. Walsh

It is appropriate that our initial subject should be the very first pilot to attain five official victories in a Vought F4U fighter, thereby becoming the first Corsair ace. Col. Kenneth Walsh saw considerable action during the assault on Bougainville early in the Solomons campaign and, with 21 Japanese aircraft to his credit, is the fourth ranking Marine ace of the Second World War. He is also the highest scoring ace of his squadron; VMF-124. This professional warrior is the recipient of the country's highest award, the Medal of Honor.

Kenneth Ambrose Walsh was born in Brooklyn, New York, on November 24, 1916. The family then moved to Jersey City, New Jersey, where he attended Dickinson High School and became an outstanding track athlete. After graduation in 1933, Walsh decided to enlist in the United States Marine Corps and spent Christmas of that year as a recruit at Parris Island in South Carolina. He then served as an aviation mechanic and radioman at the Marine Corps Base at Quantico, Virginia, until March 1936, when he was transferred to Pensacola, Florida, for flight training.

The young Private won his wings in April 1937 and was primarily stationed at Quantico from 1937 to 1941. During this period, Walsh participated in scout and observation flying on the aircraft carriers *Yorktown, Wasp,* and *Ranger,* and was promoted to Master Technical Sergeant. In 1940, the future ace married the former Beulah Barinott of Washington, DC. When the Japanese attacked Pearl Harbor, Walsh was serving with Marine Fighting Squadron 121. In May 1942, he was promoted to the rank of Marine Gunner, which is equal to Warrant Officer. Ken Walsh then transferred to Marine Fighting Squadron 124 during September 1942, and was commissioned a Second Lieutenant one month later at Camp Kearney, California.

Marine Fighting Squadron (or VMF) 124, was destined to be the first squadron to take the new Corsair into combat. Major William Gise was the Commanding Officer, and in January 1943, VMF-124 went to New Caledonia, in the Loyalty Islands, aboard an unescorted passenger ship. Their new Corsairs, however, were loaded on freighters and sent to Espirito Santo in the New Hebrides Islands, with a destroyer escort. The planes were quickly assembled and the men of VMF-124 worked hard to familiarize themselves with the new fighters. During this time the new planes were flown from dawn to dusk and the inexperienced fliers had many mishaps bringing the number of Corsairs available for duty down to 20.

Ken Walsh almost lost his life before seeing action when the Corsair he was flying deadsticked into the Pacific Ocean after a power failure. The heavy fighter quickly sank beneath the waves, taking its pilot with it. Fortunately, Walsh managed to free himself after a frantic struggle and bobbed to the surface not a moment too soon.

Ken Walsh was the very first Corsair ace having scored his fifth victory on May 13, 1943 as a member of VMF-124. He is sitting in his F4U-1A Corsair. (Defense Dept. Photo [Marine Corps])

These are the pilots of VMF-124, the very first squadron to take the Corsair into combat. Photo was taken in February 1943 with one of the new Corsairs in the background. The men are, from left to right: Top row: Capt. Quilty, Lt. English, Lt. Bedford, Lt. Newman (Medical Officer), Lt. Cannon, Lt. Mutz. Middle row: Lt. Franklin, Lt. Lamger, Lt. McDowell, Lt.

Spencer, Lt. Kenneth Walsh, Lt. Raymond, Lt. Kuhn, Lt. Johnston, TSgt. Shelton, Lt. Pearson, Lt. Taylor. Bottom row: Capt. Brewer, Lt. Kaseman, Lt. Rood, Lt. Finn, Maj. Gise (Commanding Officer), Lt. Crowe, Capt. Hart (Intelligence Officer), Lt. Hartsock. (Lt. Col. Kenneth Walsh, USMC [Ret.])

On the morning of February 12, 1943, VMF-124 arrived at Guadalcanal with 24 Corsairs. Two days later the inexperienced Marine pilots joined Army fighters in escorting Army and Navy bombers on a raid on the Japanese airfield of Kahili on Bougainville. The result was the disastrous "Saint Valentine's Day Massacre" when 50 Zeroes shot down two PB4Y bombers, two P-40 Tomahawks, four P-38 Lightnings, and two F4U Corsairs. One of the Corsairs shot down a Zero but crashed into his victim head-on. This was the last time the Japanese were able to beat the men of VMF-124. The final records indicate that this unit destroyed 78 enemy planes and lost only 11 planes and three pilots during the entire Solomons campaign.

The Japanese sent a force of 58 Mitsubishi Zero fighters and Val dive bombers sweeping down the Solomons on April 1, 1943, during "I operation" and an enormous dogfight ensued with Walsh and VMF-124 in the middle. The future ace shot down two Zeroes followed by a Val in rapid succession. He was then ordered to R&R (Rest and Recuperation). Upon his return, "Knobby" Walsh as his squadron mates called him (because comic strip prize fighter Joe Palooka had a manager called "Knobby" Walsh) was in the air on the following day. On May 13, he destroyed three more Zeroes, thereby becoming not only the first Corsair ace but the first in VMF-124.

By August 15, Walsh had become a double ace with 10 victories to his credit. On that day First Lieutenant Kenneth A. Walsh led a division of four Corsairs from Munda on New Georgia to the vicinity of Vella Lavella to prevent the Japanese from

Capt. Ken Walsh is shown on Munda, New Georgia, during August 1943 examining wrecked Japanese Zero-Sen fighter planes in this autographed photo. (Lt. Col. Kenneth Walsh, USMC [Ret.])

bombing our troops and ships. As they approached the bombers, the Marines were jumped by 30 Zeroes from 10,000 feet and the ace quickly picked out one of the attackers as his 11th victim. The Japanese pilot turned and twisted but could not shake off the Corsair and its determined pilot. Five miles later the Zero crashed into the Pacific. As Walsh turned back toward the dogfight, he ran into a flight of nine Val dive bombers and, although outnumbered, he attacked them from below and sent two of them down to join the Zero in its watery grave.

The intrepid pilot was now surrounded by Vals and Zeroes bent on avenging the death of their comrades. With his right wing peppered with 20mm cannon shells, hydraulic lines severed, stabilizer in shreds, and right tire blown, Walsh managed to elude his pursuers and sped for home. When he landed at Munda, his Corsair was so badly damaged that it was junked as a total wreck!

Marine Ace "Knobby" Walsh experienced his wildest dogfight on August 30, 1943, and his outstanding performance on that day earned him his country's highest award for heroism, the Medal of Honor. It all started at 11 o'clock in the morning, when VMF-123 and VMF-124 joined forces with Army P-39 and P-40 fighters to escort four-engined B-24 bombers in a raid on Kahili airfield on Bougainville. This airfield was the center of fierce Japanese air resistance in the Solomons. Walsh and VMF-124 took off from Guadalcanal and landed in the Russell Islands for refueling and briefing.

President Franklin D. Roosevelt congratulates Ken Walsh after presenting the ace with the Medal of Honor. Mrs. Walsh, the former Beulah Barinott, smiles proudly on this happy occasion during November of 1943. (U.S. Naval Historic Center)

At 1:30, they were in the air again, but as the armada climbed for altitude, Walsh's aircraft developed supercharger trouble. He signaled his wingman, W.P. Spencer, to go on without him and the Corsair ace dropped out of the formation and landed at Munda with his underpowered fighter. Under such conditions it was perfectly excusable for the pilot of a crippled airplane to "sit out" the raid, but Ken Walsh thought otherwise. He quickly arranged for another Corsair and within minutes was in the air again in a borrowed airplane.

Speeding toward Kahili at full throttle, it was not long before he sighted specks in the distance and assumed that they were the B-24 bombers. As he approached he discovered that the specks consisted of about 50 Zeroes closing in on the B-24 formation. The flak from Bougainville was extremely dense but the daring Marine plunged through it and caught one of the straggling Zeroes. Walsh waited until he was within 300 feet of his victim and then exploded the unsuspecting Japanese fighter into oblivion. As he sped through the pulverized wreckage of his latest kill, the aggressive pilot sighted another straggler and, within seconds, the second Zero for the day went down in smoke. The remaining Zeroes discovered the culprit and surrounded the lone Corsair. With sheer determination, Walsh broke through the enemy cordon and dived into the B-24 formation just in time to break up a concentrated Zero attack on the bombers.

This photograph shows Ken Walsh between two propeller blades decorated with Japanese flags. At this time the flier was a quadruple ace with 20 victories. (U.S. Marine Corps Photo)

He then used the Corsair's great power to climb up out of range of his pursuers. There were so many enemy fighters in the sky over Bougainville on that day that the Marine ace found it impossible to keep any one plane in his sights long enough to make another kill. Corsairs, Army fighters, and Zeroes milled about in an accelerated frenzy while the bombers droned onward toward the target.

Capt. Kenneth Walsh with his crew chief. The plane number was chosen despite superstition. Walsh scored the 20 kills shown during the Solomons campaign and attained his 21st victory over Okinawa. Photo was taken during June 1945 on Okinawa following 21st air victory. The crew chief is Sergeant Harry Ross of Cincinnati, Ohio. (Defense Dept. Photo [Marine Corps])

As Walsh struck again and again with relentless fury, he heard a distress call on his headset from another group of bombers in serious trouble, over Baga Island near Vella Lavella, with no fighter protection. Without hesitation, "Knobby" sped to the rescue and arrived in time to catch several Zeroes lining up for a six o'clock low attack on the "big friends." A short burst at long range into a Mitsubishi wing root blew up the third victory for the day.

Again maneuvering into position, Walsh put the Corsair into a tight turn and sent another Japanese fighter into the sea trailing thick smoke. As the big Corsair straightened from the turn, it was boxed in with Zeroes on both sides. Walsh tried a series of sharp turns but the attempt was futile; the experienced Japanese naval pilots stuck like glue. Cannon shells ripped through the Corsair wings, leaving gaping holes in the structure. The engine was also hit several times but the American was determined to fight it out and continued his zigzag course until the fuel pressure dropped and the engine began losing power.

It was 30 more miles back to Munda and it was becoming apparent that Ken Walsh would never make it as the cannon shells continued to pepper the Corsair. The engine now belched smoke and long white fingers of gasoline streamed from the cowling. As the Zeroes closed in for the *coup de grace,* a P-40 and a Corsair came to the rescue while the last shells pounded the dying Corsair.

Captain Walsh stands on the wing of the late-model Corsair (an F4U-4) with which he shot down his 21st victory over Okinawa on June 22, 1945. At this time, he was Operations Officer of VMF-222. (Defense Dept. Photo [Marine Corps])

With speed almost down to the stalling point, Walsh nosed the borrowed Corsair down toward the water to ditch his smoking wreck. He jettisoned the canopy and as the craft bounced on the first wave, the ace jumped before the second wave crashed over the cockpit and swallowed the riddled wreck. Walsh was exhausted but unhurt as he floated with his Mae West in the shark-infested waters.

At 5:00 that afternoon a group of Navy Seabees rescued the ace and he spent the night resting in a hospital in newly captured Vella Lavella. The next morning

After 28 years of service, Lieutenant Colonel Kenneth Walsh retired from the U.S. Marine Corps in January 1962. Photo taken just prior to the event. (National Archives)

Ken Walsh hitched a ride on an LST back to Guadalcanal and thereby ended his first tour of duty and his most harrowing combat experience.

Ordered to return to the United States, Ken Walsh was awarded the Medal of Honor by President Roosevelt on February 8, 1944, and promoted to Captain the same day. Two months later, the hero was assigned to the Naval Air Station at Jacksonville, Florida, as a flight instructor.

Captain Walsh was transferred to the Philippine Islands in April 1945, for his second tour of combat duty and served there and in the Okinawa campaign as Operations Officer of VMF 222. Ken Walsh destroyed his 21st and final victim when he shot down a Zero near Okinawa while flying a late-model Corsair.

After V-J Day, Walsh decided to remain in the service and continue his career. In March 1946, he was assigned to the Bureau of Aeronautics and three years later he joined the First Marine Aircraft Wing at El Toro, California, as the Assistant Engineering Officer, Marine Aircraft Group 12.

Captain Walsh went to Korea on July 15, 1950, as Assistant Engineering Officer with Marine Transport Squadron 152 (VMR-152). He served there until July 1951, during which time he accomplished flight missions (R5D/C-54 aircraft) in Korea, ranging from flying combat cargo to airvac (air evacuation of wounded personnel). In April 1952, the ace was Marine Liaison Officer for Aircraft Material and Maintenance with Commander, Air Force, Atlantic Fleet. In 1955 he was promoted to the rank of Major and later became the Commanding Officer, VMR-152, Third Marine Aircraft Wing. He became a Lieutenant Colonel in 1958 (October) and was stationed in Japan as the First Marine Aircraft Wing Maintenance Officer from January 1959 until April 1960.

Colonel Walsh retired from the United States Marine Corps in January 1962, after over 28 years of outstanding continuous service to his country. Kenneth Walsh now lives in California with his wife and two sons, Kenneth Ambrose, Jr., and Thomas Francis.

In addition to the coveted Medal of Honor, Colonel Walsh holds the Distinguished Flying Cross with six gold stars, the Air Medal with 14 gold stars, the Presidential Unit Citation with one bronze star, the Army Distinguished Unit Citation with emblem, the Good Conduct Medal with one bronze star, the American Defense Service Medal, the American Campaign Medal, the Asiatic-Pacific Campaign Medal with four bronze stars, the World War II Victory Medal, the Navy Occupation Service Medal with Asia Clasp, the National Defense Service Medal, the Korean Service Medal with one silver star and one bronze star, the United Nations Service Medal, the Philippine Liberation Ribbon with one bronze star, the Philippine Presidential Unit Citation, and two Korean Presidential Unit Citations.

No greater tribute could be paid to Ken Walsh than when the Marine Corps referred to the ace as "the Fighting Irishman of Marine Aviation."

Donald N. Aldrich

VMF-215—the "Fighting Corsairs"—was one of the most active squadrons in the Solomons campaign and served with great distinction in the final assault on

Rabaul. The "Fighting Corsairs" officially destroyed a total of 137 enemy aircraft and had more than its share of aces. We have selected three outstanding members of VMF-215 who contributed considerably to the success of this unit by shooting down 60 Japanese aircraft—almost half of the squadron total!

The first outstanding member of VMF-215 is Captain Donald N. Aldrich, the fifth leading ace in the United States Marine Corps, who shot down every one of his 20 victories while more than 200 miles from the nearest friendly airstrip. He

Captain Donald N. Aldrich shot down all of his 20 victories while more than 200 miles from the nearest Allied field. (Defense Dept. Photo [Marine Corps])

loved airplanes and was a natural flier who always remained with the bombers rather than wander off in search of more victories during the heat of battle.

Aldrich was born in Moline, Illinois, in 1918, but when he was one year old, the family moved to Chicago. Ever since Donald could remember, he wanted to be a pilot. This was quite natural because his father, Lyell Aldrich, was a mechanical engineer and a private pilot. He owned a Waco biplane, and father and son would go flying at least once each week. By the time Donald was 12 years old, he had

This trio from VMF-215 the "Fighting Corsairs" destroyed 60 Japanese planes, nearly half of the squadron total! From left: Bob Hanson, 25 planes; Don Aldrich, 20; Harold Spears, 15. The uniform was typical for tropical flying. (Defense Dept. Photo [Marine Corps])

almost 100 hours in the air. While in his junior year at Fonger High School in Chicago, Donald's father died and the Waco was sold.

Upon graduation, young Aldrich decided to follow his father's profession and he enrolled at the Armour Institute of Technology to study engineering. After two years of college, he could not resist the burning desire to fly. He quit school and took a job in the office of the Visking Corporation, a sausage casing manufacturer, in order to earn flying money. The air-minded youth spent every spare moment at Ashburn Field in Chicago and worked out in a Piper Cub owned by Royal Schaefer, his friend and flying instructor.

After logging about 70 hours of solo time in the Cub, he longed to fly bigger and faster aircraft. He had married recently and found that his job had no promise of rapid advancement for a stable career. Don decided to kill two birds with one stone; he would join the Army Air Corps and in this way would have a steady job with a career full of advancements and he would be able to do what he wanted most in life—fly! His wife, Marjorie, agreed and the future ace applied for enlistment after quitting his job. It was 1940; the United States was not yet desperate for fliers and had restrictions against married men. As a result, Donald Aldrich was rejected by the recruiting officer. The Royal Canadian Air Force had no such restrictions and were eager to accept volunteers from the United States. Don went to Canada in February 1941, and won his RCAF wings in the following November.

Instead of sending him to a combat area, the RCAF made Aldrich an instructor and he spent a year teaching recruits in North American Harvard trainers. At last the ban against married men was lifted by the United States and Aldrich rushed home and secured a commission in the Marine Corps in October 1942. Four months later, he was on his way overseas with VMF-215, the "Fighting Corsairs" squadron. After serving at Midway and Hawaii, Aldrich headed south to the Solomon Islands and action.

On August 26, 1943, while escorting bombers, he was attacked by several Zeroes. The Japanese shooting was most accurate and Aldrich found his Corsair was full of gaping holes and receiving serious damage. Furthermore, his body was hit with flying shrapnel from the exploding cannon shells. Instead of leaving the dogfight, however, he remained with the bombers and through his superior piloting he not only assisted in driving off the Japanese fighters but even succeeded in shooting down one Zero!

During another bomber strike in the Solomons on September 2, 1943, the guns in one wing sustained damage and could not be fired. Undaunted, Don Aldrich pressed the fight on the enemy attackers, drove them off, and shot down one Zero in flames with only half of his armament functioning.

Aldrich ended his first combat tour with five victories, which classified him as an ace. His second combat tour was uneventful, but during his third combat tour he ran his string of victories up to 20 by shooting down 15 aircraft in less than one month while protecting the bombers on raids over Rabaul!

On January 28, 1944, Donald was occupied with his job of protecting the bombers over Rabaul when the Japanese came out in force. While absorbed with sending one of the enemy to his doom, Aldrich was jumped by six Zeroes. He did not see the attackers until it was too late and 20mm shells were already tearing into the rugged Corsair. Suddenly, a shell exploded in the cockpit, sending razor-sharp pieces of jagged shrapnel deep into his shoulder and leg. Aldrich, instead of breaking away and speeding for home, turned and attacked his pursuers.

The Japanese pilots were caught by surprise and Don Aldrich shot down three more Zeroes in rapid succession. The last Mitsubishi erupted into flames after a

Capt. Donald Aldrich was awarded the Navy Cross in 1945. He was scheduled to lead his own squadron when the war ended and the assignment was cancelled. (Defense Dept. Photo [Marine Corps])

short burst at long range. Captain Aldrich then nursed the Corsair for 200 miles back to Torokina airstrip on Bougainville, where he landed with no flaps, one flat tire, and 105 bullet holes in the aircraft. His great flying ability and the ruggedness of the Corsair enabled the wounded ace to walk away from the landing.

One week later saw Aldrich back in action, where he shot down two more Zeroes on February 7, 1944. Two days later he gained his 20 victory to conclude his combat career.

The 180-pound, six-foot ace was awarded the Distinguished Flying Cross, Purple Heart, Navy Cross and Gold Star. On seven different occasions his Corsairs were riddled with holes from nose to tail by Zero cannon. Twice he brought planes home damaged beyond repair. Don Aldrich was twice wounded by 20mm shells exploding in his cockpit. Captain Donald N. Aldrich died while engaged in the activity he loved best. On May 3, 1947, he perished in a plane crash in his native Chicago.

Harold L. Spears

The second famous member of VMF-215 who fought through the Solomons campaign up to Rabaul was Captain Harold L. Spears. His 15 official victories places him 10th on the list of United States Marine Corps aces.

Born in Portsmouth, Ohio, on December 31, 1919, Harold grew up in Ironton, Ohio, where the family moved when he was quite young. While a senior football star at Ohio University, young Spears decided to apply for flight training in the U.S. Naval Reserve. He enlisted on July 30, 1941, and by October 13 of the same year was assigned to active duty. He completed preliminary flight training at the Naval Reserve Aviation Base in Kansas City, Kansas, on December 3 and was then sent to New Orleans and Corpus Christi, Texas, where he completed his flight training. Spears was commissioned a Marine Reserve Second Lieutenant on August 21, 1942, and assigned to VMSB-244, which was later designated VMF-215.

The unit was ordered overseas in February 1943, and was based on Espiritu Santo, from where it attacked Japanese bases in the Solomon Islands. As the enemy began losing its foothold in the Solomons, VMF-215 moved to Munda and Vella Lavella to cover the troop landings in Empress Augusta Bay at Bougainville. During this time the Corsair was used effectively by VMF-215 to strafe enemy positions as well as to destroy Japanese aerial resistance. While in the Bougainville action, Harold Spears shot down his first four Zeroes on August 18 and 19 and September 2, 1943, for which he received the Air Medal. He was promoted to Captain in December. Spears was awarded a second Air Medal for his strafing attacks against ground targets.

By January 18, 1944, the action had moved to Rabaul. On this day, Spears became an ace when he shot down his fifth, sixth, and seventh Zeroes while escorting Army B-25 Mitchell bombers on a raid over this Japanese stronghold. Two more Zeroes went down before his blazing guns two days later and on the 22nd of that month, he shot down his 10th victim over Rabaul. On January 26, Spears destroyed his 11th and 12th Zeroes over New Britain.

Captain Spears was awarded the Distinguished Flying Cross for heroism early in 1944. He was now a division leader and on February 3, as the bombers neared their target, several groups of enemy fighters slipped between the bombers and their "little friends." Spears' division was closest to the intercepters, but the Corsairs were heavily outnumbered. Despite this, the Marine ace went after the Japanese and, with relentless fury, he broke up the attack on the bombers. During the melee he shot down two more Japanese fighters. Under virtually the same conditions, Spears destroyed his 15th Zero over Rabaul on February 7, 1944.

Capt. Harold Spears of VMF-215 scored 15 confirmed victories in Air battles over the Solomons and Rabaul. (Defense Dept. Photo [Marine Corps])

The ace was ordered to return to the United States that month and was stationed at the Marine Corps Air Station, El Toro, California. On November 1, 1944, Spears was integrated into the regular Marine Corps and planned to make a career for himself in this outstanding service. He was assigned to VMF-462 as a flight officer at El Toro, pending another tour of duty in the Pacific. On December 6, 1944, the ace had just completed a routine flight and was in the process of landing when the craft smashed into the ground, killing him.

The death of Captain Spears was a great loss to the war effort because he was recognized as a flier with great ability and contributed immeasurably to the success of the "Fighting Corsairs."

Presentation of combat decorations on November 20, 1943 on the Vella Lavella airstrip included the presentation committee, from left to right: Lt. R. E. Clark, Maj. R. E. Owens, Jr., Maj. J. L. Neefus, and Lt. Col. H. H. Williamson, while the recipients were, from left to right: Lt. L. F. Deetz (Gold Star), Lt. B. P. O'Dell (Air Medal), Lt. D. R. Moak (Air Medal), Capt. Don Aldrich (Purple Heart), Lt. D. E. McCall (Air Medal), Lt. Robt. M. Hanson (Air Medal), Lt. T. M. Tomlinson (Air Medal), Lt. O. Keith Williams (Air Medal), and Lt. C. S. Stidger (Purple Heart). Bob Hanson's bandaged hand was injured in a freak accident, according to Col. Williams, who was there: "I was standing on a revetment one day at Munda air strip watching 215 and 221 scramble to intercept some Japs. Hansen began his takeoff from one end of the strip and another pilot was taking off from the opposite end. There was no "tower control," they hit head-on doing around 70 miles per hour. Both left wings hit; 100 gallons of high-octane exploded. Hansen had his left hand exposed and I think he lost a finger or two in the crash, thus the bandage. . . ." (Defense Dept. Photo [Marine Corps])

Robert M. Hanson

The most famous pilot of VMF-215 and the third leading Marine Corps ace was Medal of Honor winner Robert M. Hanson. This outstanding flier became a legend when he shot down 20 enemy aircraft in only six consecutive flying days!

"Butcher Bob" Hanson was born in Lucknow, India, on February 4, 1920. He was the son of Reverend and Mrs. Harry A. Hanson, Methodist missionaries

Bob Hanson smiles for the photographer in November 1943 on Vella Lavella just before taking off for a raid on Bougainville. The ace's F4U-1 waits in the background. Defense Dept. Photo [Marine Corps])

in the Far East. Bob Hanson spent his early life in Lucknow but returned to the family home in Newtonville, Massachusetts, to attend junior high school. He later returned to India, and his interest in athletics prompted him to become light heavy-weight and heavyweight wrestling champion of the United Provinces.

In the spring of 1938, Hanson bicycled his way through Europe on his way back to the United States where he planned to attend college. In fact, the future ace was in Vienna during the Anschluss when Germany occupied Austria. Bob Hanson was attending Hamline University in St. Paul, Minnesota, when the Japanese struck at Pearl Harbor. He decided to enlist for naval flight training in May 1942, and won his wings and a Marine Corps commission as Second Lieutenant on February 19, 1943, at Corpus Christi, Texas. By June of 1943 he was a First Lieutenant and in the South Pacific with VMF-215 in the Northern Solomons campaign.

Hanson completed two tours of duty in the Bougainville area during the autumn of 1943. Despite the fact that he was eligible to return home after his first tour, he elected to remain on duty in his eagerness to continue flying. He also reasoned that on the second and third tours, his combat experience would make him far more valuable. He was right. ''Butcher Bob'' destroyed a total of only five planes on his first and second tours but shot down 20 planes during his third tour!

The ace's outstanding action during the Bougainville landings occurred on November 1, 1943, in the early afternoon over Empress Augusta Bay when Hanson spotted six Japanese torpedo bombers preparing to attack the ships of the American landing force. Single-handed he drove through the enemy formation and broke up the attack. He then returned and harassed the enemy bombers until they were forced to jettison their lethal cargo. During this action, Robert Hanson shot down one of the Kates. A short while later, his flight encountered between 20 and 30 Zeroes and Kates and the men of VMF-215 shot down five. Hanson destroyed two of these, but the rear gunner of a Kate damaged his Corsair so badly that he was forced to ditch the fighter into the bay. The landing was safe and the ace climbed into his rubber boat. Bob drifted in the bay for several hours until, late in the afternoon, he sighted part of the task force off Cape Torokina and padded frantically toward it. A destroyer picked up the downed flier after he had spent six hours in the boat. A few days later he was back at Vella Lavella with the ''Fighting Corsairs'' again.

With the Bougainville landing secured, the action now moved to Rabaul. VMF-215 moved to Torokina Airstrip in December 1943, in preparation for the strikes at the Japanese stronghold. Bob Hanson elected to stay with his buddies and started his third combat tour. As soon as he arrived, his daring tactics and total disregard for danger and death became well known. Hanson was truly a master of individual aerial combat and has often been called the ''Marines' One-Man Air Force.'' It was during this action around Rabaul that he earned the name of ''Butcher Bob.''

During his very first flight into the Rabaul area, Hanson shot down five Zeroes on January 18, 1944. The ''Fighting Corsairs'' were escorting North American Mitchell bombers on a ship bombing run in Simpson Harbor when a force of 70 Japanese fighters headed for the bombers. The ''Fighting Corsairs'' promptly attacked and an enormous dogfight developed. ''Butcher Bob'' sped into the center of the huge enemy formation and when he emerged he was a double ace with five more victories!

On his second and third flights, Hanson shot down one and three Japanese aircraft respectively. The ace's fourth flight was another bombing raid over Simpson Harbor on January 24. Hanson found himself surrounded by enemy fighters and cut off from his squadron. The lone Corsair struck at the Zeroes with such devastating fury that he not only eluded a certain death but shot down four Zeroes and forced the Japanese to break off their attack on the bombers. "Butcher Bob" was on his way to becoming the Marine Ace of Aces. His next sortie added three more to the growing score and he now had 21 victories.

In the late afternoon of January 30, VMF-215 escorted Grumman TBF Avenger torpedo bombers to the Rabaul area and protected the bombers as they sank a 3,000-ton Japanese tender. Of the 21 Japanese planes shot down during this action, Hanson destroyed four to bring his total to 25. His last 20 victories were scored in only 13 days!

First Lieutenant Robert M. Hanson was in great spirits as he prepared to take off in his Corsair on the morning of February 3, 1944. It was the day before his 24th birthday and his third tour of duty would be over in a few days. The ace had planned to go to the United States for a well-earned rest and then return to the South Pacific to continue his phenomenal career. The task on that morning was to escort bombers to Rabaul and strafe gun emplacements near Cape St. George on the island of New Ireland, northeast of Rabaul.

During the strafing runs, the ground fire increased in intensity with each successive dive. Hanson put his Corsair into a shallow dive aimed at the ground targets and the Japanese returned his fire with great vengeance. Suddenly, the six wing guns ceased firing, but the Corsair remained on its course. The nose then rose slightly and the "bent-wing bird" raced across the target and out over the waters of St. George's Channel. Still it maintained its earth-bound attitude: lower, lower, then a tremendous splash. When the churned waters were still once again, the pilot and his aircraft were not to be seen. The ocean had swallowed the brave American and a careful search of the area revealed no trace of man or machine. Apparently the withering ground fire had killed Hanson.

The Medal of Honor was posthumously awarded to the heroic Lieutenant for gallantry during the actions of November 1, 1943 and January 24, 1944. The highest United States medal was presented to Mrs. Harry A. Hanson by Major General Lewis G. Merrit on August 19, 1944.

So eventful were the last few weeks of Hanson's combat career that the news services had no time to document the intricate details of his actions. There is no doubt that, had the fatal accident not occurred, Robert M. Hanson, with his tremendous potential, would have continued to increase his score and possibly become the leading Allied ace of the war.

Wilbur J. Thomas

Of the 117 Japanese aircraft destroyed by VMF-213 in the Pacific Theatre of Operations, Wilbur Thomas is credited with 18½ victories, which places this Corsair pilot eighth on the list of United States Marine aces. The bulk of his victories were scored during a one month period of intensive activity in the Central Solomons during the hotly contested Vanguna and Rendova landings.

Wilbur Jackson Thomas was born to Mr. and Mrs. E. J. Thomas in El Dorado, Kansas, on October 29, 1920. One month before his 20th birthday, he went to Kansas City, Kansas, and enlisted in the U.S. Naval Reserve as a Seaman Second Class. Thomas then applied for flight training and graduated the course at Corpus Christi, Texas, where he was commissioned a Second Lieutenant, USMCR on August 21, 1942.

Lt. Wilbur J. Thomas downed four attackers in an air battle when jumped by seven Zeroes over Rendova. (Defense Dept. Photo [Marine Corps])

After completing the pre-operational training at Miami, Florida, in December of that year, Wilbur Thomas was assigned to the Fourth Marine Aircraft Base Defense Wing. This unit had groups at Midway, Ewa, and Samoa, and was responsible for air-sea rescue, shipping escort, search and patrol, as well as air defense for our Pacific bases. Although this was very important work, Thomas yearned to get into the battle zone where there was heavy fighting. The future ace was then transferred to Marine Aircraft Group Eleven (MAG-11), based on Espiritu Santo in the New Hebrides Islands. MAG-11 also conducted air-sea rescue and search operations, and served as a funnel through which pilots, gunners, ground crews, and aircraft flowed into the battle area. He was promoted to First Lieutenant in May 1943, but was still unhappy with his assignment.

Finally, the long-awaited transfer to the battle zone arrived and Wilbur Thomas joined VMF-213 on June 18, 1943. This squadron had just relieved VMF-124 in the Russell Islands, in order to cover the New Georgia landings.

Twelve days later his flight of Corsairs acted as top cover for amphibious landings in Wickham Anchorage on Vanguna Island. Suddenly, 15 cannon-firing Zeroes were upon them and Thomas became separated from his fellow leathernecks. The red-headed Marine found himself over Rendova and before he could rejoin his flight, seven of the Zeroes had boxed in the Corsair for an easy kill. As with most outstanding fighter pilots, Thomas turned on his attackers and placed them on the defensive. This is what Wilbur wanted—real live *action!* He maneuvered with great skill and such fierce determination that first one, then another, still another, and then the fourth Japanese fighter fell in rapid succession before his blazing guns. The remaining Mitsubishi fighters broke off the engagement and sped for home. Upon landing, Thomas had nothing to say except that "my plane performed wonderfully," thereby modestly giving the credit to his Corsair.

The Distinguished Service Cross was awarded Thomas for this outstanding performance. The citation accompanying the award, which was made in August 1943, also mentions a strafing raid on a Japanese cargo supply ship by members of VMF-213. Wilbur Thomas played an important part in this action, which left the ship burning and sinking. The citation continues with a laudatory description of the ace's skill in a dogfight, when his flight of four elements intercepted a huge formation of enemy bombers and Zeroes on July 15, 1943. Thomas was in the center of the melee and sent a bomber and a fighter down in flames. As the Corsair pulled out of its dive, he felt the sickening thuds of cannon shells. A Zero was on the American's tail blasting away. Thomas avoided the Japanese fighter with a series of sharp turns and soon placed himself in striking position. A short burst and it was all over; his third victory for the day plunged into the sea.

On July 17, 1943, "Red" Thomas and his wingman attacked seven Japanese twin-engine bombers and an undetermined number of escorting Zeroes over New Georgia. The Japanese fighters fought furiously in their efforts to keep the two Corsairs away from the bombers, but Thomas found an opening in the Zero cordon and blasted away at the bombers over Kolombangara Island and sent one of them crashing to its doom. The mere audacity of the American's attack plus his skill in eluding the Zeroes was enough to discourage the bombers, for they quickly turned and headed for home with their ineffective escort.

In addition to the Distinguished Flying Cross, Wilbur J. Thomas is the holder of the Navy Cross. He was promoted to Captain in February 1944.

Harold E. Segal

As top scorer of VMF-221, "the Wake Avengers"; recipient of three Distinguished Flying Crosses, four Air Medals, and the Purple Heart; veteran of combat duty over the Solomon Islands, Bismarck Archipelago, and Philippine Islands; and the victor of 12 aerial encounters; "Murderous Manny" Segal is number 18 on the Marine Corps list of aces.

Lt. Harold "Murderous Manny" Segal scored 12 victories with VMF-221, the "Wake Avengers," to become the squadron's top scorer. (Defense Dept. Photo [Marine Corps])

Born on September 1, 1920, in Chicago, Illinois, Harold E. Segal grew up in New York City. The family then moved to Long Island, where he graduated from high school in 1939. Harold attended Pratt Institute in New York for two years and in September 1941 he enlisted in the U.S. Naval Reserve for aviation duty. After his appointment as an Aviation Cadet in March 1942, he completed flight training in Pensacola, Miami, and Jacksonville, Florida. Upon graduation Segal was commissioned a Marine Reserve Second Lieutenant and designated a Naval Aviator in October 1942. In May 1943, Harold was assigned to VMF-221 and he joined the squadron in the New Hebrides on Espiritu Santo. The unit then moved to Guadalcanal to participate in the battle for the Solomon Islands.

Segal scored his first kills on June 25, 1943, over the coast of New Georgia, when VMF-221 intercepted a flight of Bettys with a Zero escort. "Murderous Manny" destroyed one bomber and one fighter during this action.

During another patrol flight on July 11 Segal became separated from his squadron when they encountered more Japanese bombers and fighters. The intrepid flier quickly joined another lone Corsair and together they attacked an armada of 15 Mitsubishi Bettys and an equal number of Zeroes. His job was to stop the bombers and Segal was determined to turn them back regardless of the consequences. During the first pass the Corsair received several cannon shells in the engine which made it lose considerable power, but Harold kept after the bombers as the Zeroes frantically intervened. The rugged Corsair shuddered as shells exploded in the airframe. Several hit the cockpit and shrapnel wounded Segal, but he would not concede defeat and pressed the attack.

As the uneven battle progressed, the wounded pilot in the crippled fighter managed to shoot down a total of three Zeroes to become an ace, but by then the Corsair could no longer sustain flight. Segal put his "bent-wing bird" into a shallow dive and headed for a forced landing in the waters off New Georgia. Throughout his descent the Zeroes forgot the bombers and fired at the wounded pilot who was kept busy zigzagging as well as negotiating a crash landing. The landing was perfect and in a few hours Harold Segal was picked up by an American ship.

Four days later the "Wake Avengers" shot down six Japanese aircraft over Rendova, three of which were credited to Segal. On August 6 the Corsair pilot was escorting a photographic mission over Kolombangara, in the New Georgia group, when a large number of Zeroes made an effort to intercept the photo plane. Segal fought furiously until the camera plane completed the job and headed for home. Only then did the ace break off the fight. He raced for his base in a badly damaged plane but with a happy heart, for "Murderous Manny" had destroyed two more Japanese fighters.

VMF-221 moved to Munda on November 4, 1943, to aid in the Bougainville landings. The squadron was kept busy with fighter sweeps, task force covers, strafing, and long range patrols. On the morning of the 17th a Japanese air fleet of 55 Zeroes and 10 carrier bombers left Rabaul to attack eight U.S. transports and 10 destroyers in Empress Augusta Bay. An early warning post sighted the raiders, alerting a big patrol of Army, Navy, and Marine fighters. The intercepting forces included VF-17 and VMF-221. As the two armadas met the sky was full of airplanes, twisting and turning in their dance of death.

Segal darted in and out of the fracas firing at every enemy plane that crossed his gunsight. Finally the Japanese broke and sped back to Rabaul after four bombers and six fighters were shot down by the Americans. Of the 10 U.S. victories on that day, Segal was credited with three of the bombers, thus bringing his total to 10 and making the flier a double ace.

Capt. Harold E. Segal receives a Gold Star from Lt. Col. F. E. Pierce in lieu of a second Distinguished Flying Cross in April 1944. (Defense Dept. Photo [Marine Corps])

The "Wake Avengers" served as cover for bombing runs on Rabaul and other Japanese strongholds on New Britain during the early days of 1944. It was while on one of these raids on January 24 that Segal shot down two more intercepting Zeroes to bring his total to an even dozen. The Corsairs of VMF-221 destroyed 185 Japanese planes, shooting down 71 of this total during one month's fighting over New Britain.

Harold Segal was ordered home in the following month and was assigned to the Marine Corps Air Station in El Toro, California. One year later in May 1945 the ace returned to the Pacific area and joined VMF-115 at Zamboanga on the Philippine island of Mindanao. There was very little aerial activity but the squadron was kept busy strafing ground targets on the Japanese-held portions of the island and covering the beaches during amphibious operations. Segal was so proficient at strafing that he earned his third Distinguished Flying Cross and three Air Medals for his skill and daring in ground attacks. The lack of air resistance prevented him from increasing his score and it is a matter of record that VMF-115 was only able to boast of 6½ air victories.

Captain Harold E. Segal went to Manila in August 1945 and then transferred to China before he returned to San Diego on January 31, 1946. Segal was assigned to duty at the Brooklyn Navy Yard until his detachment from active service as a Captain in March. The ace remained in the Marine Corps Reserve and was promoted to the rank of Major in September 1951. He was honorably discharged on August 7, 1958.

Gregory Boyington

Unquestionably the most swashbuckling air hero of the Pacific War was "Pappy" Boyington, who led one of the toughest Marine Fighter squadrons in the Pacific Theatre of Operations. This Medal of Honor winner is the number one Marine Corps ace with 28 victories to his credit and is one of the most unforgettable characters in the history of combat aviation. No story of Corsair combat would be complete without including this amazing pilot.

Born on December 4, 1912, in Coeur D'Alene, Idaho, Gregory Boyington spent his spare time during boyhood hunting for Indian relics. This is quite understandable because he is part Sioux Indian and inherited much of the independence, bravery, and dogged determination of that proud nation. Boyington grew up to be a strong and husky youth and during his college years became Intercollegiate Wrestling Champion. During his summer vacations he worked in a mine in Golden, Idaho, in order to pay for his tuition and subsistence. Turning to a military career, Boyington joined the Marine Corps and soon became an aviation cadet. Promotions came at regular intervals and by 1941 he was an instructor at the Naval Air Station in Pensacola, Florida, with the rank of Captain. The tough Marine had earned the nickname of "Rats" at this time.

In September 1941 Boyington resigned his commission in the Marines to join the American Volunteer Group or "Flying Tigers" in China. The Japanese invasion of China was in full swing and the "sleeping giant" desperately needed experienced fighter pilots. They offered $675 per month plus a bonus of $500 for each enemy plane shot down. The U.S. Government wholeheartedly approved of Boyington's decision to join the group. A Dutch ship carried the flier across the Pacific to Java, then Singapore, and Toungoo in Burma. Finally, one month later, he arrived in Kunming, China.

The Flying Tigers were equipped with Curtiss P-40 fighters and the expert pilot scored his first victory on his second flight when he shot down a Nakajima 96 fighter in flames. By the time Boyington attained his sixth victory, the AVG was scheduled

Major Gregory "Pappy" Boyington, the Ace of Aces of the Marine Corps, scored a total of 28 victories. Boyington's Bulldog tenacity and determination is clearly reflected in his facial expression as he prepares to lead the Corsair pilots on a mission against the Japanese. (U.S. Marine Corps Photo)

to become part of the Army Air Corps. The vast majority of AVG pilots joined up, but not "Pappy." Once a Marine, always a Marine. Upon his return home during the summer of 1942, Boyington applied for readmittance to the Marine Corps. Red tape and indecision delayed his induction until November, when the tough flier sent a blistering telegram to the Assistant Secretary of the Navy.

Three days later he was on his way to San Diego to join his beloved Marines. By January 1943 Boyington was again crossing the Pacific Ocean this time on the S.S. *Lurline* heading for Noumea, New Caledonia. He was finally based at Espiritu Santo in the New Hebrides as assistant operations officer of the coral airstrip. Needless to say, Boyington despised this administrative post and strongly agitated for a combat assignment. Finally, on April 20, 1943, he was placed in command of VMF-122 equipped with Grumman Wildcats. His task was to escort dive bombers in the "Slot" from Guadalcanal to Bougainville. He completed his first combat tour without seeing as much action as he had anticipated.

After this first tour he was ordered to rest in Sydney, Australia. He returned to Espiritu Santo in June and was scheduled to resume command of VMF-122, which had just been supplied with brand-new Corsairs. But fate was against the flier, however, because on the seventh of the month he broke his ankle while wrestling and was forced to go to a hospital in Aukland, New Zealand, while VMF-122 went into combat under the command of Major Herman Hansen, Jr. Returning to Espiritu

"Pappy" Boyington's first command was VMF-122 based on Guadalcanal in the spring of 1943. He is shown here briefing his pilots before the squadron embarks on a raid on Japanese shipping in the "Slot." (Defense Dept. Photo [Marine Corps])

Santo Boyington was shifted from squadron to squadron as a temporary replacement and after six of these transfers with little or no flying, he decided he had enough of this nonsense. From July 26 to August 11 he took over VMF-112.

During August 1943 the spirited pilot talked the Group Commander into forming a temporary fighter squadron composed of the many pilots in the area who were waiting for permanent assignments. In fact, it has been said that these pilots were rejected by the various commanders because they were rowdy, undisciplined, and potential troublemakers! The new unit borrowed the designation VMF-214 from a squadron that had just completed a combat tour and Boyington assumed command of the squadron on September 7.

In view of the fact that the new CO was the oldest active fighter pilot in the Marine Corps, the men called their leader "Gramps" or "Grandpappy" and this gradually evolved to "Pappy." This name has been used so often that his first name has almost been forgotten. VMF-214 moved to Munda in the Russell Islands on September 12 and, with only three pilots with combat experience, "Pappy" led his squadron on their first mission four days later.

Taking off with 20 Corsairs from Munda, first mission for VMF-214 was to escort about 150 Grumman TBF torpedo planes and Douglas SBD dive bombers

The men of VMF-122 discuss the strategy and tactics of aerial warfare after returning from a successful sortie against the enemy. Boyington, center, encouraged discussions of this type because an exchange of ideas improved the efficiency of the unit. Notice the inflatable life jackets, called "Mae Wests," worn by the pilots. (Defense Dept. Photo [Marine Corps])

Before Boyington assumed leadership of VMF-214 in September 1943, the squadron had been known as the "Swashbucklers" and had seen action since mid-March. "Swashbucklers" of the original VMF-214 posed for this photo in Hawaii just before embarking for the Southwest Pacific in early 1943. Second row standing: Luthi, Deetz, Pettit, Hollmeyer, Sigel, Rankin, O'Dell, Hoover, Scarborough, Williams. First row sitting: Schaefer, Carpenter, Lanphier, Miller, Burnett, Ellis, Britt, Pace, Kraft, Bernard, Cavanaugh,

Fidler, Hazelwood. Major William H. Pace became the "Swashbuckler's"
commanding officer on July 12, 1943; however, on August 6, as he was easing
his shot-up Corsair back to base, the engine seized while approaching the
airstrip. Pace bailed out at once; however, his chute had just begun to open
when he struck the shallow water and sustained fatal injuries. (Lt. Col. O.
Keith Williams, USMC [Ret.])

With a beautiful Bent-Wing Bird in the background, the members of VMF-214 "Swashbucklers" take time out from the war to pose for a photographer in the Russell Islands during July 1943. The pilots are: Fourth row: Pettit, McCall, Hollmeyer, Sigel, Scarborough, Knipping, Fidler, Rankin. Third row: Cavanaugh, Synar, Hatch, Miller, Burnett, Bookman, Eisele, Carpenter. Second row: Hernan, Hazelwood, Moak, Bernard, Williams, Jensen, Dunbar. First row: Taylor, Tomlinson, Deetz, Hunter, Curran, O'Dell. Dave Rankin was an All-American end from Purdue in '39 and '40. Vince Carpenter was captain of the Yale track team and a world-class hammer thrower. On August 27, 1943, five "Swashbuckler" Corsairs and three from VMF-215, led by Maj. Robert G. Owens, were on their way to attack the Kahili airfield on Bougainville when the formation was scattered by a violent tropical storm over the target.

In addition, the antiaircraft fire was intense and accurate, which dampened the attack. Lt. Alvin Jensen, who had been promoted in the field from the rank of technical sergeant, fought his way to the Japanese airfield alone and strafed the bombers on the runways and tarmac until 13 were in flames. Al Jensen was awarded the Navy Cross for this feat. Major Owens and his wingman broke through the clouds later and witnessed the results of Jensen's solo attack. After two tours of combat, VMF-214 "Swashbucklers" went for R&R in Sydney, Australia, on August 31, 1943. Upon its return to Espiritu Santo the "Swashbucklers" was broken up because it was short several pilots. The squadron number was given to Maj. Boyington and became the "Black Sheep." Some "Swashbuckler" pilots were sent to the U.S. mainland but most were sent to join other squadrons, such as VMF-215, to replace lost pilots. (Lt. Col. O. Keith Williams, USMC [Ret.])

to Ballale, just west of Bougainville. As the armada neared its target it was jumped by 40 Zeroes. Boyington led his wingman, Moe Fisher, into the oncoming Japanese before the enemy could reach the bombers. Each man quickly shot down a Mitsubishi fighter during the initial attack and then the squadron leader dived to protect the bombers from those Zeroes which had broken through the Corsairs. He fired at the nearest Zero at point blank range and the Japanese exploded. Boyington was so close to his victim and flying so fast that he could not avoid speeding through the shattered fragments. Pieces slammed into the Corsair, severely denting the rugged fighter, but it remained in flying condition.

Suddenly the air was clear of the enemy, and with the mission completed, the Corsairs turned for home. Boyington spotted a Zero skimming the wavetops, but as he nosed down toward the enemy he suspected a trap and quickly reversed his direction to find another Zero bearing down on him. As the two adversaries raced toward each other at breakneck speed there was time only for a short burst of fire and ''Pappy'' shot first. His third victory of the day went crashing into the Pacific. He again reversed direction and found the low-flying Zero racing for home. The powerful Corsair closed the gap and a well-placed burst at long range splashed the enemy. As ''Pappy'' climbed to rejoin his squadron he caught several Zeroes attacking a crippled Corsair straggler. Without hesitation he plunged to the attack. Boyington's intended victim zoomed straight up and ''Pappy'' followed, firing all the way. Just as the Corsair began to stall the Zero burst into a ball of flame for Boyington's fifth victory of the day! Running low on fuel, he was then forced to return to Munda.

The outstanding performance of ''Pappy'' and VMF-214 on their first mission earned them fame overnight. With this fame they picked up a nickname: ''Boyington's Bastards.'' However, propriety dictated that this could not be used in official communiques. It was changed to the ''Black Sheep'' because originally no one wanted the pilots who now formed the highly successful VMF-214.

On October 17, 1943, the ''Black Sheep'' escorted Grumman Avengers in a raid on Kahili airfield. The mission was completed without any enemy interference despite the fact that over 60 Japanese fighters were parked on the airfield. Upon his return to Munda, Boyington ordered the 26 Corsairs refueled and he then led his men back to Kahili. During his service in China and in the Pacific Theatre, ''Pappy'' studied Japanese and could converse in the language of the enemy.

As the Corsairs flew over the airfield, Boyington made radio contact with the Japanese and, in their own language, he insulted, berated, and challenged them to come up and fight him. The enraged Japanese ran to their Zeroes and soon 30 enemy fighters were climbing to meet the ''Black Sheep.'' Boyington exploded the lead Zero, then turned slightly and flamed a second as the frantic pilot bailed out. Making a 360-degree turn, the veteran pilot fired into his third victim and sent it down in a ball of flame. The entire action took 30 seconds and during this time 20 Japanese planes were shot down with no Corsair losses! This outstanding action is mentioned in Boyington's Medal of Honor presentation.

Shortly after this episode the ''Black Sheep'' were helping Army Bell Aircobra and Lockheed Lightning fighters escort Consolidated B-24 bombers when the mission ran into a fierce tropical storm. The Lightnings and Aircobras turned back but Boyington kept his men on the job of protecting the huge bombers. In appreciation, the U.S. Army planned to give the ace the Silver Star. However, the Navy rejected the idea. This would have been the only medal awarded to Boyington during his duty in the Pacific despite his outstanding service!

"Pappy" Boyington loved to sleep. In fact, on long missions the ace rigged the control stick with rubber bands and string so that he could doze periodically while his "bent-wing bird" flew on an even keel with no one at the controls. He also smoked in the cockpit during sorties, as did several other great aces, with total disregard for rules and regulations. In November the six week tour was over and VMF-214 was rotated out of the battle area to Sydney, Australia.

Upon his return the following month, Boyington was selected by General Ralph Mitchell to lead the fighter sweeps against the Japanese stronghold of Rabaul. The first sweep took place with "Pappy" commanding a mixture of 31 Corsairs, 23 Warhawks, and 22 Hellcats. This armada was not successful because it apparently scared the majority of Japanese pilots into staying on the ground rather than risk their precious planes against this huge force. The next sweep, on December 23, was more successful with only 48 fighters. These accounted for 30 enemy aircraft while only three American planes were lost. Boyington shot down four of the total.

On Christmas Day VMF-214 took off from Vella Lavella just before noon and joined several other squadrons in escorting 15 Consolidated B-24 bombers on a raid on Rabaul. This raid was significant because it was planned to destroy the enemy's

"Black Sheep" Corsair taxis for takeoff.

ability to counterattack an American task force which was striking at Kavieng, New Ireland. When the Japanese interceptors appeared Boyington led his 63 escorting fighters through the center, which made the enemy turn tail and run. "Pappy" selected one of the nearest Zeroes and flamed the naval fighter with a short burst. The pilot bailed out into the waters of St. George's Channel. Climbing slightly, the CO smoked his second Zero, whose pilot followed his buddy with his parachute.

Suddenly, the ace felt the unmistakable thuds of 20mm cannon shells on his Corsair and rolled out of the line of fire. Boyington then maneuvered for the upper hand and sent his attacker crashing into the waves. After the bombers laid their eggs, Boyington turned for Rabaul when he spotted nine Tony fighters. The intrepid flier sneaked up to the formation, picked off "tail-end Charlie," and then raced for home.

By January 3, 1944, Major Gregory Boyington was in poor health and looked forward to the end of his third tour of duty, which was over on the 28th of the month. The constant physical and mental strain and unsanitary conditions were too much even for the indestructible "Pappy." His ears were infected and he had sores on his chest and armpits. He could not sleep well and was in a highly nervous state. On that morning he took off in a borrowed Corsair from Bougainville to lead a fighter sweep over Rabaul. His own "bent-wing bird" was undergoing repairs but another great Marine ace, Marion Carl, let Boyington have his Corsair.

At this time Boyington's score stood at 25 and Carl wanted to give the old-timer a crack at beating Eddie Rickenbacker's and Joe Foss' record of 26 victories

"Pappy" Boyington, leader of the "Black Sheep" squadron VMF-214, waves to the photographer as he prepares to take off from a jungle airstrip in his Vought Corsair. Notice the hastily stenciled identification number 883. (U.S. Marine Corps Photo)

before his tour was over. Everyone knew that their leader was worn out and Captain George M. Ashmun insisted on going along as Boyington's wingman to protect the great leader. At 7:45 Boyington sighted 10 Japanese planes below and ordered an attack. He dived with his wingman and at 400 yards he destroyed his 26th victim. As the two Corsairs attempted to return to their squadron they were cut off by 20 more Zeroes which dived from above. Maneuvering as one unit, the pair of Corsairs then destroyed another Zero each but the odds were too great. Ashmun's plane had been hit by the Japanese cannon and was smoking badly. The Japanese lined up and one by one they peppered Ashmun with machine guns and cannon. Boyington joined the procession, firing wildly at the massed Zeroes and brought down number 28.

As Ashmun crashed into the waves the Zeroes concentrated on Boyington, who turned and sped for safety on the deck. Cannon shells sprayed the Corsair and one struck the fuel tank, which erupted into a ball of flame. The ace climbed for altitude as the flames licked at the cockpit and by the time he reached 200 feet, the heat became unbearable. Time was running out, so "Pappy" kicked the stick forward and crashed through the closed canopy. His parachute opened just as his feet touched the waters of St. George's Channel. With his Mae West full of holes, scalp torn, left ear almost severed from the head, arms and shoulders full of shrapnel, bullet in his leg, left ankle shattered by a cannon shell, and shrapnel in his groin, the Marine

"Pappy" Boyington discussing his Corsair with Chance Vought field representative and troubleshooter Ray DeLeva. Field reps proved an important factor in helping pilots get the most out of their planes. Boyington never flew with victory flags on his aircraft because the Japanese would "gang up" on him if he did; these flags were glued on for publicity photo purposes. (Ling-Temco-Vought)

Side View

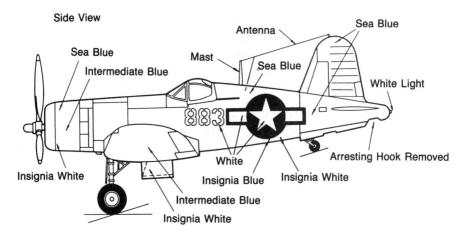

Sea Blue

Antenna

Mast

Sea Blue

Sea Blue

White Light

Sea Blue

Intermediate Blue

White

Insignia White

Insignia Blue

Insignia White

Intermediate Blue

Insignia White

Arresting Hook Removed

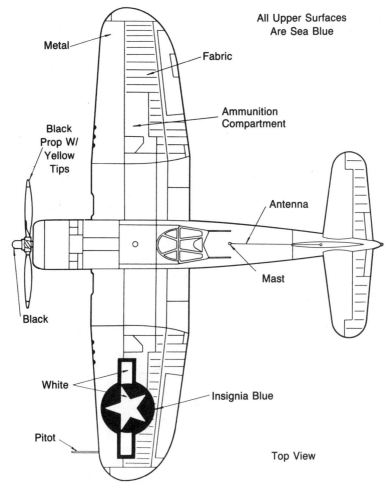

Metal

Fabric

All Upper Surfaces
Are Sea Blue

Ammunition
Compartment

Black
Prop W/
Yellow
Tips

Antenna

Mast

Black

White

Insignia Blue

Pitot

Top View

VMF 214 F4U-1D Corsair flown by Maj. Gregory "Pappy" Boyington.

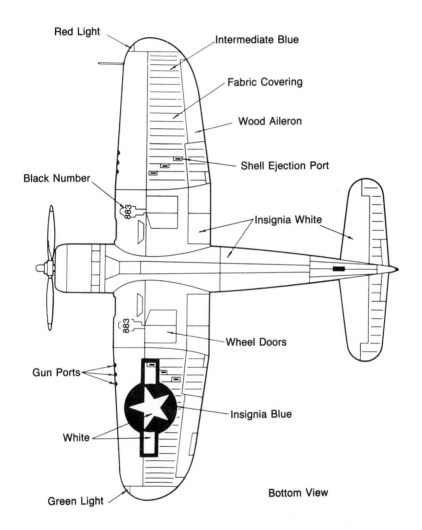

Red Light

Intermediate Blue

Fabric Covering

Wood Aileron

Shell Ejection Port

Black Number

883

Insignia White

883

Wheel Doors

Gun Ports

Insignia Blue

White

Green Light

Bottom View

Ace of Aces treaded water helplessly as the Zeroes strafed him for 15 minutes without success. The Japanese pilots finally stopped trying to kill the man who made life so unbearable for them and returned to Rabaul when the "Black Sheep" reappeared. The men circled their fallen leader until their fuel ran low and were forced to return to base.

Catalina search and rescue planes were sent to pick up the Major but they were too late. After drifting for eight hours Boyington was captured by a Japanese submarine and was taken to Rabaul. His wounds were neglected for 10 days and the ace was finally sent to Japan. Poor diet and hard labor reduced his weight from 190 pounds to an unbelievable 110 pounds. Boyington was classified as a "Special Prisoner" and not a prisoner of war, thus word of his capture was not relayed to the outside world. As a result he was given up as dead and Captain Lawrence H. Howe succeeded him as leader of the "Black Sheep."

When the Japanese surrendered, the ace "returned from the dead" after 20 months of captivity and was given a tumultuous welcome. President Harry S. Truman presented the Medal of Honor to Boyington and General Archibald A. Vandergrift gave "Pappy" a belated Navy Cross. The Marine received a hero's welcome complete with a ticker tape parade up Broadway in New York City. Upon his return to civilian status the hero found it difficult to adjust to a normal life and began drinking to excess. Fortunately, Boyington had enough strength and courage to fight this creeping alcoholism and finally settled down. His knowledge of wrestling enabled him to earn a living as a referee. After starring in a television series about the Second World War he married Dee Tatum in 1959.

Ira C. Kepford

All of the aces we have met thus far were U.S. Marine fliers who bore the lion's share of the bloody battle for the Solomons and Rabaul. Very few U.S. Navy squadrons were engaged in this area and these were virtually all land-based. Of the Navy units which participated in the campaign, there is one squadron that took a very active part in the fight for Bougainville and Rabaul and emerged most successful. This was VF-17, and the outstanding ace of this outfit, who flew a Corsair in the Solomons with 17 official victories to his credit, was former football star Ira Cassius Kepford. He became the fifth leading ace of the U.S. Navy in only five months of combat duty while engaged in the campaign to crush Rabaul.

"Ike" Kepford was born in Harvey, Illinois, on May 29, 1919 and is the son of George Raymond and Emma McLaughlin Kepford. After completing high school, Kepford enrolled in Northwestern University in Evanston, Illinois, where his athletic prowess enabled him to become a star halfback on the Northwestern football team. While still a student, "Ike" Kepford joined the U.S. Naval Reserve on August 18, 1941. He arranged to be honorably discharged on April 29, 1942, in order to accept an appointment as a Naval Aviation Cadet. Following flight training at Corpus Christi, Texas, and Miami, Florida, Ensign Kepford won his wings on November 5, 1942. In January of the following year, Kepford was assigned to newly formed Naval Fighting Squadron 17 (VF-17), in Norfolk, Virginia. This unit, under the command of Lieutenant Commander John T. Blackburn, was the first Navy squadron to see action with the Vought Corsair fighter.

"Tommy" Blackburn's squadron included 10 ensigns and two fliers with combat experience. During their period of familiarization with the new Corsairs, VF-17 became known as "Blackburn's Irregulars" and official naval parlance called the men "high-spirited" because of their hell-raising antics with the powerful Corsairs.

Lt. Ira C. Kepford of VF-17, the Jolly Rogers, is the fifth ranking Navy Ace with 17 victories. (U.S. Navy Photo)

They ran trucks off the road by flying inverted down the highway, staged dogfights over racetracks, hedgehopped over official ceremonies making the Navy brass "hit the dirt," and buzzed residential areas, which resulted in howling protests. Blackburn insisted that his unit would give the Japanese real trouble if they could ever get into combat. His wish was granted and the unit was finally assigned to the aircraft carrier *Bunker Hill*. However, the orders were changed and VF-17 arrived at Ondonga, New Georgia, in October 1943 as a land-based unit due to alleged inadequacies of the Corsair landing gear. "Blackburn's Irregulars" adopted a "Jolly Roger"—skull and crossbones on a black flag—for their unit insignia, which was painted on each side of the engine cowl.

Captain John T. Blackburn in 1955. He led VF-17, "Blackburn's Irregulars," in the Solomons during the winter of 1943. (U.S. Navy Photo)

VF-17 distinguished itself in the Pacific fighting by shooting down eight Japanese airplanes for each Corsair they lost. The unit flew an amazing 8,577 combat hours and their score in the Solomons stood at 156 planes destroyed and five transport ships and barges sunk, with a loss of only 12 pilots. The squadron also boasted of 12 aces, more than any other Navy unit. All this in only 76 days of combat! During one five-day period "Blackburn's Irregulars" shot down 60 Japanese aircraft!

On November 11, 1943, one month after VF-17s arrival in the area, Ensign Kepford participated in a top cover assignment protecting a United States Task Force which included the aircraft carriers *Bunker Hill* and *Essex*. As the ships steamed into Empress Augusta Bay, all hell broke loose. The sky was filled with bursting antiaircraft shells and Japanese aircraft. Suddenly 18 Japanese torpedo bombers launched an attack on the aircraft carriers and were dangerously close to their targets when Kepford and the "Irregulars" dived to the rescue.

In the first pass the Corsair pilots shot down all but one of the enemy, and he was quickly destroyed on a subsequent attack just as he was about to launch his torpedo. During the course of the long mission protecting the carriers, many of the Corsairs landed on the decks to refuel and rearm despite the fact that, officially, this was not sanctioned. During this battle Kepford pressed home his attacks through intense antiaircraft fire and destroyed four enemy aircraft and damaged a fifth out of a formation of thirty. He was awarded the Navy Cross for his outstanding performance that day.

By the time the squadron moved to Piva airfield on Bougainville in January 1944, Kepford had been promoted to the rank of Lieutenant Junior Grade. On the 29th of the month "Ike" Kepford was part of a bomber escort on a strike against Tobero airfield, which protected the Japanese base of Rabaul. The defending Japanese fighters greatly outnumbered the Corsairs, but the former football hero led his wingman in an attack on 12 enemy airplanes with the result that Kepford himself shot down four of his adversaries. The U.S. Navy awarded the ace the Gold Star in lieu of a second Navy Cross for his expert marksmanship and courage during the mission.

Ira C. Kepford's closest brush with disaster occurred on Saturday, February 19, 1944. VF-17 had been based on newly won Bougainville for less than a month and they were forced to operate under adverse conditions. The food was poor, the pilots lived in hastily erected tents located in a sea of mud, and to make matters especially unbearable, the many Japanese soldiers who remained in the surrounding jungle were always sniping at the American airmen. In the air the pilots wore only a pair of shorts, tennis shoes, and a summer coverall flying suit because of the heat. The squadron executive officer, Lieutenant Commander Roger Hedrick, led 20 of "Blackburn's Irregulars" on a strafing mission to Rabaul at 8:00 in the morning of the fateful day and Kepford was assigned as part of a flight of four aircraft to act as top cover for the attack.

As the four-plane division approached the coast of New Ireland, Kepford's wingman, Ensign Don McQueen, was forced to turn back because of engine trouble. Under normal conditions Kepford would also be compelled to leave the flight because the skies above Rabaul were infested with Japanese planes and no Allied plane was permitted into the area without his wingman. Flight leader Hedrick made an exception

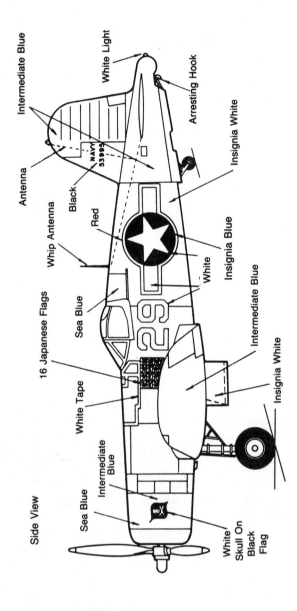

F4U-1D flown by Ira Kepford, VF-17.

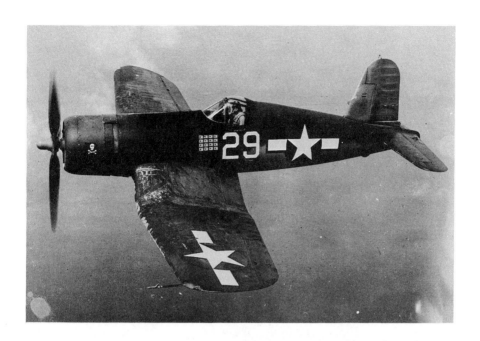

Ike Kepford's No. 29 shown at rest and in flight with both sides of the craft visible. Note that victory flags appear on both sides of the fuselage. Also note the "Jolly Roger" squadron insignia on the engine cowl. (National Archives)

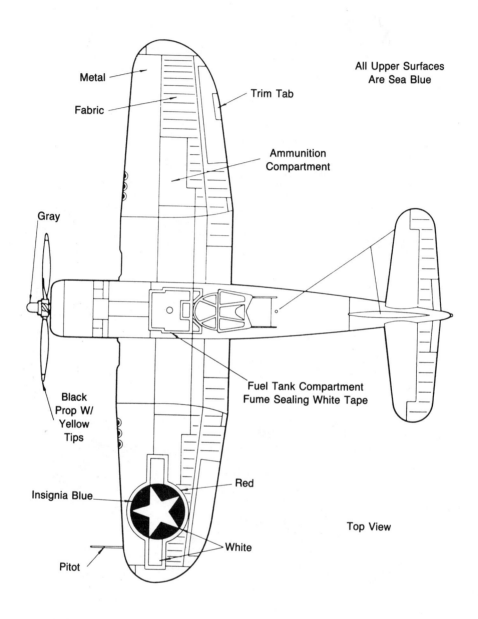

Metal

Fabric

Trim Tab

All Upper Surfaces
Are Sea Blue

Ammunition
Compartment

Gray

Fuel Tank Compartment
Fume Sealing White Tape

Black
Prop W/
Yellow
Tips

Insignia Blue

Red

White

Top View

Pitot

F4U-1D flown by Ira Kepford, VF-17.

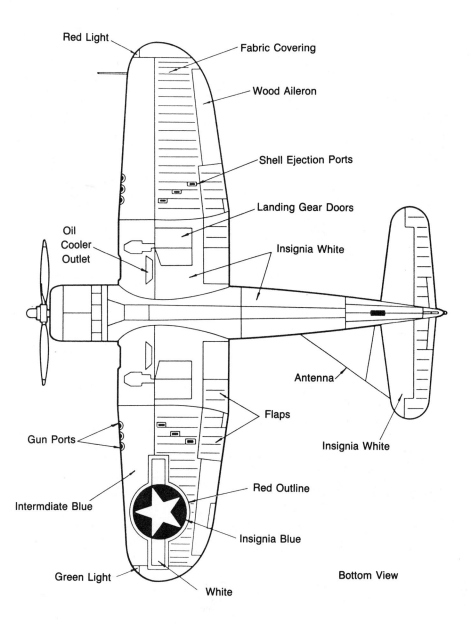

Red Light

Fabric Covering

Wood Aileron

Shell Ejection Ports

Landing Gear Doors

Oil
Cooler
Outlet

Insignia White

Antenna

Insignia White

Flaps

Gun Ports

Red Outline

Intermdiate Blue

Insignia Blue

Green Light

White

Bottom View

F4U-1D flown by Ira Kepford, VF-17.

in Kepford's case but when the unit arrived at the target area the ace was ordered to return to Bougainville due to the strong Japanese resistance.

As Kepford lost sight of the squadron on his return to base he spotted a lone Japanese Rufe seaplane below and dived to the attack. The first burst of fire from the six wing guns sent the enemy craft into the ocean trailing dense smoke. Climbing

U.S. Navy Lieutenant Ira C. Kepford shot down 17 Japanese aircraft and is one of the leading Navy aces of the Solomons campaign. He was a brilliant backfield football star with the Northwestern University team before the war. Today he is a top executive in the Liggett Rexall Drug Company. (National Archives)

to regain precious altitude he suddenly became aware of a Japanese fleet of Zero and Tojo fighters flying at 16,000 feet directly above his flight path to Bougainville. Realizing the impossible odds, Kepford dived to wavetop level and turned away from the oncoming armada, hoping that he would not be detected. Too late; two Zeroes and two Tojos left the formation and attacked the lone Corsair for what they considered an easy kill. The ace opened his throttle and banked away from the impending doom swooping down upon him. The diving enemy fighters had gained tremendous speed during their dive and therefore, as the leading Zero opened fire, Kepford "popped" his flaps only 50 feet above the water and made the Japanese pilot overrun his target. As the Zero flashed by, Kepford opened fire for a split second and shattered the Mitsubishi stabilizer, sending the plane crashing into the waves.

Members of V-17, Jolly Rogers, in formation. Men were hell-raisers and became known as "Blackburn's Irregulars" because "Tommy" Blackburn was the squadron Commanding Officer. (U.S. Navy Photo)

The remaining Japanese fighters now had the Corsair neatly boxed with two Tojos on the right and the Zero on the left. Furthermore, "Ike" Kepford found himself speeding in the wrong direction and with every second of this chase he flew closer and closer toward Japanese held islands. In desperation the American forced the throttle beyond its normal full power position cutting in the water injection system, which had recently been installed in the Corsairs of VF-17. The big fighter shuddered and then surged forward with an unbelievable burst of power. After several minutes Kepford noticed that his pursuers were dropping farther and farther behind but he could no longer continue on his incorrect course. In a sudden maneuver he turned violently to the left in an effort to escape the trap but the Zero began to turn inside of the Corsair's flight path. As he skimmed over the water, Kepford fought to keep the Corsair from stalling while the Zero pilot began firing.

Suddenly the wingtip of the Japanese fighter struck the water and the craft cartwheeled across the surface, disintegrated, and sank. The two Tojo fighters, meanwhile, had been sucked wide during the turn and now fell so far behind the Corsair that they gave up the chase. Kepford landed the riddled Corsair on Bougainville at noon with only a few drops of fuel left in the tank. He was shaking badly and had perspired so profusely throughout the harrowing ordeal that the perspiration running down his legs had actually changed his tennis shoes from white to green! Kepford's use of water injection was one of the first applications of this device in combat and actually saved his life.

On the following month Kepford was returned to the United States and assigned to the Fleet Air Command at Alameda, California. That June saw the ace transferred to Fighting Squadron 84 until December of 1944, when Kepford was attached to the Staff of Commander Fleet Air, West Coast. He remained at this assignment throughout the remaining period of hostilities. On May 1, 1945, Kepford was promoted to the rank of Lieutenant. After the Japanese surrender, and a period of terminal leave, the ace was released from all active duty on November 7, 1945. He was transferred to the retired list of the U.S. Naval Reserve with the rank of Lieutenant Commander on the basis of combat citations on June 1, 1956.

In addition to the decorations previously mentioned, Ira C. Kepford was the recipient of the Silver Star, three Distinguished Flying Crosses, Air Medal, Unit Commendation to VF-17, and American Defense Service Medal.

4

Korea:
Night Ace

The invasion of South Korea by North Korean Communist troops on June 25, 1950, triggered the Korean War that eventually involved the United Nations and the U.S., as well as Red China. By the summer of 1952 the United Nations' counteroffensive had regained considerable territory, including the recapture of the very strategic Kimpo Airfield. The operation of jet aircraft from this and other airfields, such as the Taegu strips, added to the success of the U.S. jet fighters against the MiG-15. Hard-pressed, the North Koreans then resorted to psychological warfare to lower the efficiency and morale of American and other United Nations troops.

Using the Russian-built YAK-18 aerobatic trainer and LA-11 fighters, the oriental communists routinely flew over U.S. troop concentrations, bases, and airfields in nocturnal nuisance raids. These single-engine, propeller-driven airplanes usually appeared about 2:00 in the morning and dropped small bombs for no strategic or tactical purpose. The objective of these raids was to keep the troops awake at night running to shelters or to assigned emergency posts, thereby destroying their tranquil sleep and replacing it with mind-shattering excitement. By the time the men were ready for action at their antiaircraft guns, the raiders were but a barely audible drone in the distance.

Constant repetition, night after night, of "Operation Bed Check Charlie" was having its desired effect on the UN personnel and was on the verge of reducing their combat efficiency. "Bed Check Charlie" had to be stopped and U.S. jet fighters were deployed to erase the nuisance flights. Unfortunately, the raiders were too slow and too agile for the speedy jets and easily turned inside and away from their powerful pursuers. It was then decided that the only possible way to combat the communist menace was to employ agile propeller-driven aircraft equipped with search radar and heavy armament. Since there was no U.S. Air Force unit in the area with both suitable aircraft and adequate night fighting training, the authorities looked to the U.S. Navy, which was operating late-model Corsairs most effectively, for assistance.

On June 25, 1953, five U.S. Navy Corsair fighters were transferred to Kimpo airfield from the carrier USS *Princeton*. These craft were part of Composite Squadron Three (VC-3), all-weather Night Fighter-Detachment D (Dog), and ordered to operate in close liaison with the Fifth Air Force. Their aircraft were Vought F4U-5N Corsairs, one of the last variants of this famous Second World War fighter, and were numbered 21 to 25. To make these dark blue craft even more inconspicuous in the blackness, the star insignia and all white identification and instruction lettering received a light overspray of the dark blue paint, which gave the normally white areas of these F4U-5N fighters a non-regulation pale blue color.

The Vought F4U-5N night-fighting and all-weather Corsairs of Detachment D were under the command of Lieutenant Guy P. Bordelon Jr., whose personal Corsair was number 21. He christened this aircraft *Annie-Mo* in honor of the pet name he used for his wife, the former Ann Craig Taylor. Prior to his assignment to Kimpo, Bordelon successfully completed many combat missions in Korea with bombing and rocket strikes against ground targets in all kinds of inclement weather.

Guy Pierre Bordelon Jr. was born in Ruston, Louisiana on February 1, 1922, to Guy P. and Thurla Hearn Bordelon. After attending Louisiana Tech. and Louisiana State University, he volunteered for Naval Aviation Training in 1942 as World War

The Korean War's only triple threat ace poses for a Navy photograph in his dark blue Corsair. Lt. Bordelon is the only U.S. Navy ace, the only night fighter ace, and the only propeller-driven fighter ace of the Korean Conflict. Notice the four red stars emblazoned on the cockpit side signifying the four night victories with which he was credited at this time. (U.S. Navy Photo)

II raged on three continents. Upon his commissioning as Ensign in May 1943, he served as Intermediate Flight Instructor with North American SNJ Texans until May 1945. Bordelon then completed training as a combat team leader and from October 1945 to July 1948, he was a member of the ''Sundowner'' squadron, VF-11. During this time he was promoted to the rank of Lieutenant. Additional courses at the Advanced Training Command prepared Bordelon for his role as F4U Corsair advanced flight instructor. He then became Administration Officer on staff of the Chief of Naval Air Advanced Training.

At the start of the Korean Conflict, Bordelon served on the staff of Commander Cruiser Division three on the USS *Helena*. His positions included Staff Intelligence Officer, Assistant Operations Officer, and Assistant Logistics Officer. He was then made Officer in Charge of Night Fighter Detachments on the carrier *Princeton*.

Four days after their arrival at Kimpo, the VC-3 Corsairs scrambled into the inky blackness after a flight of ''Bed Check Charlies'' that had been reported near the capital city of Seoul. Using the airborne APS-19A search radar, the instrument-laden Corsairs vectored in on their quarry. Bordelon then spotted the shadowy forms of the ''bandits'' and closed in for the kill with visual sighting. The moment the

Navy ace Guy P. Bordelon chats with members of his ground crew upon landing after a sortie. Items of interest on the F4U-5N in the background are the conical flash guards on the cannon muzzles, the exhaust flare deflector screen on the fuselage side above the pilot's head, and his personal insignia of Annie-Mo *on the side of the cowl. Note also the 15 small bombs signifying ground attack missions. (U.S. Navy Photo)*

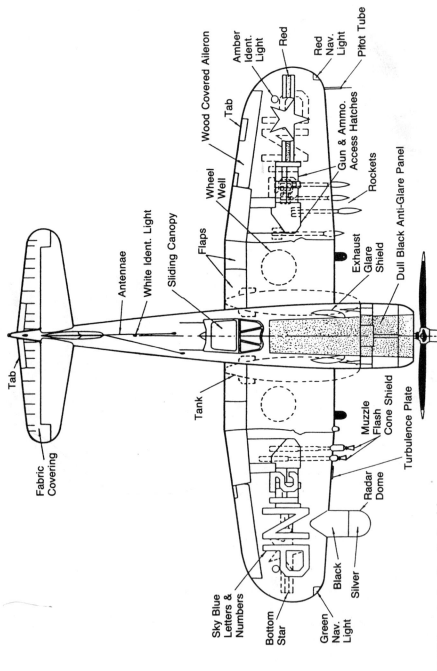

Wood Covered Aileron

Amber Ident. Light

Red

Red Nav. Light

Pitot Tube

Tab

Gun & Ammo. Access Hatches

Rockets

Wheel Well

Antennae

White Ident. Light

Sliding Canopy

Flaps

Exhaust Glare Shield

Dull Black Anti-Glare Panel

Tab

Tank

Muzzle Flash Cone Shield

Turbulence Plate

Fabric Covering

Sky Blue Letters & Numbers

Bottom Star

Radar Dome

Green Nav. Light

Black

Silver

F4U-5N flown by Lt. Guy P. Bordelon.

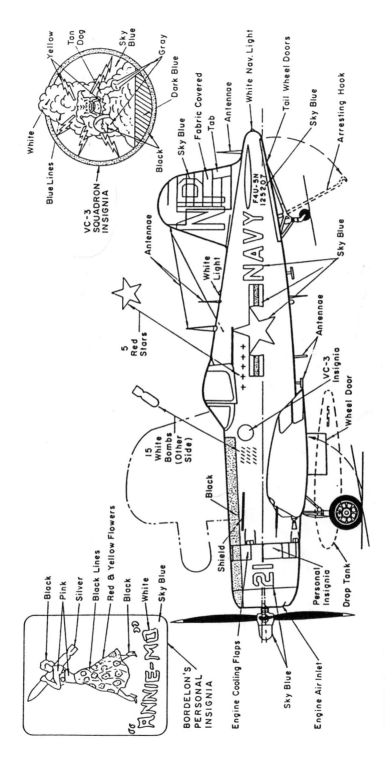

VC-3
SQUADRON
INSIGNIA

White
Blue Lines
Yellow
Tan
Dog
Sky Blue
Gray
Dark Blue
Black
Sky Blue
Fabric Covered
Tab
Antennae
White Nav. Light
Sky Blue
Tail Wheel Doors
Arresting Hook

Antennae
White
Light
Sky Blue

5 Red
Stars

Antennae
VC-3
Insignia
Wheel Door

15 White
Bombs
(Other
Side)

Black
Shield

Black
Pink
Silver
Black Lines
Red & Yellow Flowers
Black
White
Sky Blue

BORDELON'S
PERSONAL
INSIGNIA

Engine Cooling Flaps
Sky Blue
Engine Air Inlet
Personal
Insignia
Drop Tank

F4U-5N flown by Lt. Guy P. Bordelon.

103

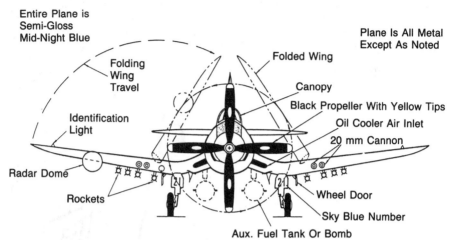

Entire Plane is
Semi-Gloss
Mid-Night Blue

Plane Is All Metal
Except As Noted

Folding
Wing
Travel

Folded Wing

Canopy

Black Propeller With Yellow Tips

Identification
Light

Oil Cooler Air Inlet

20 mm Cannon

Radar Dome

Rockets

Wheel Door

Sky Blue Number

Aux. Fuel Tank Or Bomb

F4U-5N flown by Lt. Guy P. Bordelon.

*Upon his return to the carrier Princeton from Kimpo Airfield, Lt. Bordelon received a tumul-
tuous welcome and the flight deck was decorated with signs indicating that the crew and officers
were proud of the triple threat ace. (U.S. Navy Photo)*

Lt. Guy Bordelon stands proudly at attention during the ceremony for presentation of the Navy Cross to the ace. This award is second only to the Medal of Honor and can be seen beneath his pilot's wings. (U.S. Navy Photo)

Lieutenant pressed the firing button, the communist pilot started to take evasive action but a slight kick of the rudder pedals directed the 20mm shells into the frail YAK-18 monoplane, which erupted into a giant fireball. Although momentarily blinded by the flash, the American peered into the murky darkness and finally sighted another "Bed Check Charlie" speeding for the 38th parallel on a zig-zag course. Bordelon slammed the throttle forward and was soon pumping shells into the second YAK-18, which joined its fellow intruder on a hillside north of Seoul.

On July 1, Bordelon scored again. This time he destroyed two LA-11 fighters south of the city of Suwon, and on the 16th of that month the Lieutenant became an ace by shooting another LA-11 out of the black sky. Bordelon's success was accomplished during only 15 nocturnal interception sorties and his victories came with such rapid succession that they so dampened the enthusiasm of future "Bed Check Charlie" intruders that not one Red ventured over United Nations territory in the nights that followed.

Ten days after Bordelon's fifth victory a truce was signed that ended the fighting, so Detachment D returned to the USS *Princeton*. Bordelon received a tumultuous welcome by the officers and crew of the carrier because not only was he the only U.S. Navy ace of the Korean Police Action but also the only night fighter ace and the only ace to use a propeller-driven airplane! His were the last victories scored by an American Corsair. Lt. Bordelon was presented with the Navy Cross for a job well done.

Upon the cessation of hostilities the hero served with the Military Assistance Advisory Group in France, where he instructed French Naval pilots in all-weather night fighting tactics with the Vought F4U-7 Corsair. He then became Air Traffic Control Officer at Moffett Field. Bordelon completed the General Line Officers Postgraduate Course and then served as Assistant Gunnery Officer on the carrier *Yorktown*. On July 1, 1955, he was commissioned Lieutenant Commander. In September 1959, Bordelon was attached to Airborne Early Warning Barrier Squadron, Pacific, as part of the DEW Line defense. His latest post is that of Public Affairs Officer on the Staff of Commander Manned Spacecraft Recovery Force, Atlantic.

In addition to the Navy Cross, Commander Bordelon has been awarded two Silver Stars, four Air Medals, and the highest South Korean award, The Order of Military Merit Ulchi With Silver Star.

Like every other ace who flew the Corsair to victory, Commander Bordelon has nothing but praise and affection for the classic "bent-wing bird."

The following eight photographs are an almost unbelievable sequence of an F4U-1A crash landing on the CVE 31 USS Prince William:

A. With hook extended, the Corsair settles to flight deck.

B. Engaging the arresting cable at high speed breaks the arresting hook. The plane bounces on the deck and strikes the island. The right wing shears off.

C. The fuselage breaks forward of the cockpit as the landing gear snags onto the island bulwark.

D. The wing drops into the catwalk as the fuselage settles to the deck.

E. *The landing gear snag prevents the engine from falling onto the cockpit. Flames are visible around the ruptured tank.*

F. *Flames erupt around the cockpit. Rescue teams on station.*

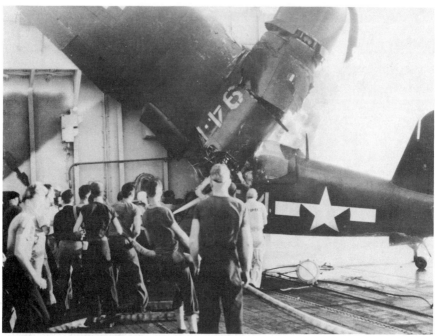

G. *The pilot is trapped in the cockpit. as the fuselage continues to settle.*

H. *The landing gear still holds the engine and left wing aloft as foam is sprayed into cockpit and fuselage rests on deck. The pilot was injured, but survived, attesting to the great strength of the Corsair.*

A

Fighter Organization
And Squadron Histories

The basic administrative and tactical unit of any air arm is the *squadron*. United States Navy and Marine fighter squadrons consisted of 18 aircraft prior to the Japanese attack on Pearl Harbor. The 18 aircraft were divided into six flights or sections of three planes each. The flight operated as the smallest tactical unit each with its individual leader.

As new fighter tactics were evolved during the Spanish Civil War and the Battle of Britain, the universally used three-plane flight was discarded and replaced with a two-plane tactical *element* consisting of a *leader* and his *wingman*. The wingman flew alongside and slightly to the rear of the leader. His job was to assist and protect his leader in battle; conversely, a good leader must not lead his wingman into a dangerous position.

The United States Navy and Marines were quick to adopt the two-plane element, sometimes called a *section*. When two elements are combined for a specific task they are called a *division* and one of the four pilots is designated the *division leader*. Both Navy and Marine squadron strength during the Second World War varied from two to nine or more divisions depending upon the strategic and tactical application at a given time. The standard carrier squadron still consisted of nine elements, but was subject to modification as required.

Several squadrons were combined under a central command and this combination was called a *group*. The standard U.S. Carrier Air Group consisted of four squadrons; however it could be as small as two or as large as six squadrons, again depending upon the tactical application. Pre-war groups were identified with specific carriers or Naval Air Stations. However, for the sake of flexibility, this practice was terminated during the war because the units were shifted from duty to duty as needed.

Two or more groups were combined to form *wings*. A wing governs the general air operation in a given battle area.

The entire organizational pattern was quite flexible, especially with land-based units. This proved to be an asset, especially in the Solomons campaign where extra squadrons and double-strength units were formed as needed depending upon the enemy resistance.

Marine Fighting Squadron One-One-Two (VMF-112) "Wolf Pack"

VMF-112 was formed on March 1, 1942, in San Diego under the command of Major W. J. Huffman. Major P. J. Fontana succeeded Huffman on May 11 and left Camp Kearney, California, with his Squadron for New Caledonia on October 13. The unit arrived in Noumea 15 days later and by November 2 the first echelon landed on Henderson Field, Guadalcanal, and actively engaged in the drive toward Rabaul. On March 27, 1943, Captain R. B. Frazer took command and was replaced by Major H. Hansen, Jr., on July 9. Major G. Boyington led the Squadron from July 26 to August 11, when Major H. Hansen Jr. took the unit to Miramar, California. VMF-112 was retrained for operation from aircraft carriers and was then based on the USS *Bennington*. Remaining under the command of Major H. Hansen Jr., the unit participated in the Iwo Jima and Okinawa campaigns and made air strikes against Tokyo until July 1945, when it returned to the U.S. Lt. G. Leonard took command on August 26 until the Japanese surrender. VMF-112 downed a total of 140 enemy aircraft, which makes it the third most successful Marine Fighter Squadron of the Second World War.

Marine Fighting Squadron One-Two-One (VMF-121)

This unit was the most successful Marine Fighting Squadron of World War Two with 208 official victories to its credit. The Squadron was commissioned at Quantico, Virginia, on June 24, 1941, under the command of Major S.S. Jack. During August 1942, the unit arrived in New Caledonia led by Captain L.K. Davis. One month later VMF-121 landed on Guadalcanal. The Squadron participated in the early Solomons fighting and served three tours of duty under the able commands of Lt. W.W. Wilson, Major D. K. Yost, Major J.N. Renner, Major R.L. Vroome, Captain R.E. Bruce, and Lt. H.O. De Fries. The Squadron returned to the United States with Capt. Q.B. Nelson in command in October 1943. After retraining at Mojave, California the unit sailed from Espiritu Santo aboard the aircraft carrier *Kwajalein* in June 1944 under Major W. J. Meyer. In the early autumn of 1944 the unit was based on Emirau, Bismarck Archipelago, and then moved to Peleliu in October for air strikes against Yap. Major C.H. Welch replaced Major Meyer on May 26, 1945, and Major R. Tucker took command during the following month. This Squadron returned to the United States with Lt. R.M. Loughery in charge and he remained in command until the unit was decommissioned after V-J day.

Marine Fighting Squadron One-Two-Two (VMF-122)

Organized on March 1, 1942, at Camp Kearney, California, the unit left for Espiritu Santo on November 9 under the leadership of Captain E.E. Brackett Jr.

Some pilots served with VMF-121 on Guadalcanal for several months early in 1943. On April 20, 1943, Major G. Boyington took command and the unit engaged the enemy during June and July in the New Georgia landings. Major H. Hansen, Jr., was in charge from June 8 to July 7 and was followed by Major R.B. Frazer. VMF-122 completed its tour of duty on July 23 and Major J.H. Reinburg took the unit back to Mirimar, California. After reorganizing and retraining at El Centro, California, Major Reinburg took the Squadron to Espiritu Santo aboard the SS *Hollandia* in July 1944. On the following month the flight echelon flew to Emirau and air strikes against Yap, Koror, and Babelthuap began in October. The Squadron assisted the U.S. Army during the landings at Pulo Anna in November 1944. The unit operated from Peleliu until the Japanese surrender. Major F.E. Pierce, Jr., was in command from February 1 until March 14, 1945, when Major Q.B. Nelson succeeded him. When Major Nelson was killed in action on April 16, 1945, Major D.H. Sapp took charge on May 28 after two temporary leaders. The unit is credited with 35 official victories.

Marine Fighting Squadron One-Two-Three (VMF-123)

With 56 official victories to its credit, this unit saw considerable action throughout the Pacific. Captain R.M. Baker was in charge of the Squadron when it was formed at San Diego, California, on September 7, 1942. It left for Guadalcanal on January 8, 1943, and went into action on February 4 under the leadership of Major E. W. Johnston. Major R.M. Baker led the unit again from April 2, 1943, until September 11, 1944. After serving two tours of duty on Guadalcanal, the unit moved to Munda on August 14, 1943, and in September it operated from the Russell Islands. On November 28, 1943, VMF-123 left the Solomons for the U.S. and regrouped and retrained at Santa Barbara and Mojave, California. Major E.V. Alward commanded the Squadron on the carrier *Bennington* from January 1, 1945, until he was killed in action on February 25. Major T.E. Mobley, Jr., succeeded Alward and led the Squadron on strikes against Tokyo. VMF-123 also participated in the Iwo Jima landings in March 1945 as well as the Okinawa campaign during the following month. The Squadron returned to the United States during July 1945 still under the command of Major Mobley.

Marine Fighting Squadron One-Two-Four (VMF-124)

This squadron was the first Marine unit to be equipped with Corsair fighters and it scored 78 official victories with this famous plane. The unit was organized at Camp Kearney on September 7, 1942, from the remnants of the old VMF-122, under the command of Lt. C. B. Brewer. The squadron arrived at Guadalcanal on February 11, 1943, and was led into action by Major W. E. Gise. When Major Gise was killed in action on May 13, he was succeeded by Captain C. B. Brewer. The unit saw heavy action in the Solomons campaign under the leadership of Captain Brewer, Major W. H. Pace, and Major W. A. Millington. VMF-124 participated in the Russell Islands, New Georgia, and Vella Lavella operations and scored most of its victories during these actions. Major Millington led the unit back to the U.S.

on October 13, 1943. After reorganization and retraining at Mojave the squadron shipped to Pearl Harbor aboard the *Ticonderoga*, where it transferred to the carrier *Essex* on December 28, 1944. As a carrier-based unit it then participated in the Lingayen landings in the Philippines and conducted air strikes against Tokyo. During the spring of 1945 the unit operated in the Iwo Jima and Okinawa campaigns. Under the command of Major J. M. Johnson, the Squadron returned to the U.S. once again in April 1945. After more training it embarked for Ewa, near Pearl Harbor, during September 1945.

Marine Fighting Squadron Two-One-One (VMF-211)

This Squadron was the former peacetime VMF-2 and underwent reorganization and redesignation on July 1, 1941, under the command of Major C. L. Fike. The forward echelon arrived at Wake Island on December 4 and participated in its defense under the leadership of Major P. A. Putnam. After being based on Palmyra, Ewa, and Espiritu Santo, the unit moved to the Russell Islands during October 1943. Led by Major R. A. Harvey, VMF-211 furnished close support for the Bougainville landings and by December the unit was based on Bougainville. Major T. V. Murto, Jr. led the Squadron in concentrated air strikes against Rabaul during the early spring of 1944, during which time the unit scored many of its 91 victories. Part of the Squadron moved to Green Island in March and during the following month it operated from Emirau. The Squadron united in May under the new command of Major T. P. Wojcik, who was replaced by Major S. J. Witomski on October 20, 1944. In December the unit was based on Leyte in the Philippines and covered the Ormoc and Mindoro landings. In January 1945 the unit participated in the Lingayen invasion. The following month saw the Squadron provide support for the Biri and Capul landings under the command of Major P. B. May. On March 9, 1945, the Zamboanga operation benefited from the skill and bravery of VMF-211. Major A. F. Davis took command on March 21 and led his men to support the landings at Bongao, Jolo, Malabang and Sarangani Bay.

Marine Fighting Squadron Two-One-Two (VMF-212)

VMF-212 was commissioned at Ewa on March 1, 1942, under the command of Medal of Honor winner Major H. W. Bauer. By March the forward echelon arrived at Efate. During June and July, the unit was based in the New Hebrides and New Caledonia. Operations began from Henderson Field, Guadalcanal, in September. Major Bauer was shot down on November 14 and was succeeded by Major F. R. Payne, Jr., who took the Squadron back to the United States during that month. In June 1943, Major S. B. O'Neill led the unit back to Midway and two months later landed in Espiritu Santo. The Squadron returned to the Solomons fighting in August and scored many of its 132½ victories at this time. The unit was heavily engaged in the Vella Lavella and Bougainville campaigns. In October 1943, the pilots were based at Barakoma to support the Choiseul and Bougainville operations. Major H. M. Elwood assumed command on January 1, 1944, and led the men in strikes against Rabaul from the base on Vella Lavella. After April Majors W. A. Free and

B. C. McElhany led the Squadron in continued attacks on Rabaul. By January 8, 1945, VMF-212 was based on Samar and participated in the Philippines fighting under Major Q. R. Johns. Late in the Spring, the unit flew close support missions for U.S. Army troops. Operations on Okinawa began on June 7, 1945, and the Squadron remained there, under Major John P. McMahon, until the Japanese surrender.

Marine Fighting Squadron Two-One-Three (VMF-213)

This Corsair Squadron scored the vast majority of its 117 official victories during heavy fighting in the Solomons. The Squadron was born at Ewa, Hawaii on July 1, 1942, with Capt. H. T. Merrill as CO. By March 1943, the unit was on Espiritu Santo, where it received some of the first production Corsairs. The following month saw the unit on Guadalcanal where the commanding officer, Major W. H. Britt, Jr., was killed in action on April 13. He was succeeded by Major G. J. Weissenberger, who took the unit to the Russell Islands to cover the New Georgia landings. On August 22, Major J. R. Anderson took command and the Squadron returned to Guadalcanal on September 5 for strikes against Bougainville during the early autumn. Part of the Squadron was also based on Munda during this time. Captain L. W. McCleary led the unit from October 22 to November 4, when Major S. R. Bailey took command for 11 days. Lt. E. O. Shaw was the CO when VMF-213 embarked on the *Kitty Hawk* from Espiritu Santo and sailed for home on December 9, 1943. After being reformed and retrained for carrier duty the Squadron was assigned to the carrier *Essex* on December 28, 1944. Major L. R. Smunk led the unit in the Lingayen landings in January 1945, as well as strikes against Luzon, Formosa and French Indochina. The Squadron pounded Tokyo in February with Major D. E. Marshall in command. Attacks on Okinawa occupied the Squadron during March 1945, until the unit returned to the United States.

Marine Fighting Squadron Two-One-Four (VMF-214) "Black Sheep"

This unit is generally known as Pappy Boyington's "Black Sheep" and it scored many of its 127 victories while under the command of Major Boyington. Commissioned on July 1, 1942 at Ewa, VMF-214 was known as the "Swashbucklers" and included many veterans of the Battle of Midway. Captain Charles W. Somers was in command. After arriving at Espiritu Santo in February 1943, the flight echelon continued to Guadalcanal where it remained until May under Captain George F. Britt. After training in their new Corsairs on Efate during June and July 1943, the Squadron went to the Russell Islands. From July 12, Major William H. Pace led the unit in the assault on Bougainville until he was killed in action on August 6. He was succeeded by Captain J. R. Burnett, who took the Squadron to Munda. During August the Squadron broke up due to losses and the unit became replacement pilots for other Squadrons that had been shot up. The Squadron number was given to Major Boyington. Early in September, Major Gregory R. Boyington took command and the Squadron was soon known as the "Black Sheep." In November VMF-214 was based on Vella Lavella and made the first fighter sweep against Rabaul. Shortly after Boyington was shot down and captured on January 3, 1944, the Squadron returned to the United States for carrier training. Major S. R. Bailey led the men on raids over Japan and Okinawa from the aircraft carrier *Franklin* during February and March 1945. On March 19, the Japanese severely bombed the ship with great loss of life. This forced the remnant of the unit to return to the United States, where it remained until V-J Day.

Lt. Col. Walter E. Lischeid was commanding officer from July 8, 1950 to September 25, 1950. VMF-214 was deployed to Kobe, Japan on July 12, 1950. Assigned to MAG 33, 1st MAW. The unit arrived at Pusan, Korea, August 2, 1950 on board USS *Badoeng Straight* flying F4U-4Bs. Flight operations against enemy positions began immediately, making VMF-214 the first Marine squadron to fight in Korea. Before the war was over VMF-214 would complete two combat tours flying from the USS *Boxer* during their second tour.

During August, VMF-214 with VMF-323 flew constant close air support ahead of Marine and Army troops. On Aug. 10, 1950, Corsairs from VMF-214 and VMF-323 engaged in the softening up process for the invasion of Inchon. On September 16, 1950, in full view of the Marine ground forces, VMF-214 dropped napalm on Soviet-made T-34 tanks that had been moving through a village on the outskirts of Inchon. The troops cheered the Corsair pilots.

It was on September 19, 1950, that although MAG-33 was ordered to occupy the airfield at Kimpo, VMF-214 was ordered to remain aboard the carrier by Maj. Gen. Field Harris, Commanding Officer of the 1st MAW. The general wanted the Squadron to keep at the job that they had been doing so well.

Lt. Col. Walter E. Lischeid was killed in action on September 25, 1950. From September 7 to October 9, 1950, VMFs 214, 323 (carrier based), 212 and 313 (at Kimpo) flew 2,163 total sorties. On November 2, 1951, VMF-214 ceased combat operations.

Marine Fighting Squadron Two-One-Five (VMF-215) "Fighting Corsairs"

With 137 official victories, this unit is the fourth ranking Marine squadron of the Second World War. It was organized on June 3, 1942, and designated VMSB-244 (scout and dive bombing unit) but by mid-September VMF-215 had been created. It arrived at Midway in April 1943, under the command of Captain J. L. Neefus. During July, the Squadron was based on Espiritu Santo and began attacking Japanese bases in the northern Solomons. It moved to Munda on August 12, 1942. The second tour of duty began in early October on Vella Lavella. Lt. Colonel H. H. Williamson led the Squadron on strikes against Rabaul and Kavieng until December 5, when Major R. C. Owens took command until February 1944. Major J. K. Dill was CO when the unit was reformed at Turtle Bay and then moved to Emirau during the summer. The unit continued to hammer at the Japanese under the command of Major B. S. Hargrave, Jr., from early June to late August. On September 14, 1944, the Squadron moved to Guadalcanal and then left for the United States for a well-earned rest and arrived on the West Coast on October 20, 1944. The unit acted as a replacement training squadron until the end of the war.

Marine Fighting Squadron Two-Two-One (VMF-221) "Wake Avengers"

The second leading Marine fighting squadron with 185 official victories, was formed on July 11, 1941, at San Diego, California, under the leadership of Major W. G. Manley. On October 6, Major V. J. McCaul took command and led the men to Pearl Harbor two months later. On the very next day an advanced flight echelon boarded the carrier Saratoga and rushed to help in the defense of Wake Island. When this tiny island fell to the Japanese, the Squadron sped to the defense of Midway Island. On June 4, the unit lost 15 planes. The squadron leader, Major F. B. Parks, was one of the airmen killed in action on that day. After helping to save Midway, the unit moved to Ewa and then to Guadalcanal during February 1943. Following two tours of combat duty under Captain R. R. Burns and Major M. K. Peyton, they moved to Vella Lavella and covered the Treasury Island invasion during October under the leadership of Major N. T. Post, Jr. After supporting the Bougainville landings, the Squadron was based at Munda and participated in the carrier attack against Rabaul on November 11, 1943. Concluding its excellent performance in the Solomons, the unit left for San Francisco on December 14. Reorganized at Miramar and retrained at Santa Barbara for carrier duty, VMF-221 went to sea on the *Bunker Hill* in December 1944, led by Major E. S. Roberts, Jr. They raided Tokyo, covered the Iwo Jima attack, and participated in the Okinawa campaign before returning to El Centro, California, on June 9, 1945.

Marine Fighting Squadron Two-Two-Two (VMF-222) "Flying Deuces"

This Squadron was commissioned on March 1, 1942, at Midway and by September it had returned to the United States under the command of Captain R. M. Haynes. Captain M. J. Volcansek, Jr. took the unit back to Midway, from where it sailed for Espiritu Santo in July 1943. The Squadron was based on Guadalcanal on September 3, and then moved to newly won Munda from where it actively engaged in the Solomons fighting. By mid-November, Major A. N. Gordon had taken command and the men moved to Vella Lavella. During December, it participated in fighter sweeps over Rabaul. In the spring of 1944, VMF-222 was based on Emirau, from where it continued to hammer at Rabaul. Major R. T. Spurlock became the CO on April 28, 1944, and in August of that year, the unit moved to Green Island, closer to Rabaul. In January 1945, it was based at Samar and engaged in the Philippine campaign. In April 1945, Major H. A. Harwood took charge and the unit then moved to Okinawa on May 22. VMF-222 scored a total of 53 official victories during its several tours of duty.

Navy Fighting Squadron One-Seven (VF-17) "Skull & Crossbones"

This famous unit is the most outstanding U.S. Navy Squadron that participated in the Solomons campaign, where it destroyed 156 enemy planes in only 76 days! The Squadron was the first Navy unit to see action with the Vought Corsair fighter. It was organized in Norfolk, Virginia, during December 1942, under the command of Lt. Commander John T. (Tommy) Blackburn. Originally assigned to operate from the aircraft carrier *Bunker Hill*, certain alleged inadequacies with the Corsair landing gear caused the unit to be reassigned to the land-based operation of the Solomons campaign. In October 1943, they arrived at Ondonga, New Georgia. By January 1944, VF-17 was operating from Bougainville and in March, returned to the United States. It was reformed at Alameda during April 1944, under the command of Lt. Commander M. U. Beebe and after intensive training, VF-17 boarded the carrier *Hornet* in February 1945. It participated in the invasion of Iwo Jima and Okinawa. Fighter sweeps on Japanese airfields on Kyushu were the order of the day during March 1945, and the unit kept busy bombing and strafing the Japanese home islands and naval units until the surrender. VF-17 shot down 146½ more enemy planes from March 18 to April 17, 1945.

B

Corsair Targets and Losses During World War II

Sortie Targets:

Enemy airfields	10,210
Other military ground targets	32,770
Land transportation	2,818
Miscellaneous land targets	2,177
Harbor areas	2,095
Armored warships	263
Unarmored warships	245
Merchantmen (more than 500 tons)	799
Merchantmen (less than 500 tons)	3,172
Ships (type unknown)	23

Losses:

Air combat	189
Enemy anti-aircraft	349
Operation during action sorties	230
On other flights	692
Aboard ship or on ground	164

C

Vought F4U Corsair Development during World War II

XF4U-1	Prototype
F4U-1	First production model
F4U-1A	Blown canopy, raised cockpit
F4U-1B	Procured for British Royal Navy (Corsair I)
F4U-1C	Four 20mm cannon replacing machine guns
F4U-1D	Twin pylons for fuel tanks or bombs (Corsair II)
F4U-1P	Photoreconnaissance
XF4U-2	Special radar-equipped night fighter
F4U-2	Night fighter radar, autopilot
XF4U-3	Projected turbosupercharger
XF4U-4	Prototype with new engine, four-blade propeller
F4U-4	Basic production model
F4U-4B	Procurred for British Royal Navy
F4U-4C	Four 20mm cannon replacing machine guns
F4U-4N	Radar-equipped night fighter
F4U-4P	Photoreconnaissance
F3A-1	Brewster-built F4U-1A (Corsair III)
F3A-1D	Brewster-built F4U-1D
FG-1	Goodyear-built F4U-1A (Corsair IV)
FG-1D	Goodyear-built F4U-1D
FG-1E	Radar-equipped
FG-3	Turbosupercharged engine
F2G-1	3,000-hp engine, fixed wing
F2G-2	3,000-hp engine, folding wing

D

Decorations and Awards

The highest United States award for bravery is the Medal of Honor. The Army and Navy versions differ. U.S. Navy and Marine heroes are awarded the decoration shown here. The bronze medal is suspended from a blue ribbon which encircles the neck. It is awarded for "gallantry and intrepidity at the risk of life above and beyond the call of duty." (Defense Dept. Photo [Marine Corps])

Awarded only to the U.S. Navy and Marine personnel, the Navy Cross is the second highest award in the United States. The bronze medal hangs from a blue and white ribbon and is awarded for "extraordinary heroism in connection with military operations against an armed enemy." Its Army equivalent is the Distinguished Service Cross. (Defense Dept. Photo [Marine Corps])

Awarded for "exceptionally meritorious service to the Government in a duty of great responsibility," the Distinguished Service Medal is the third highest United States award. This blue and gold medal with white star is the Navy and Marine version and hangs from a blue and yellow ribbon. (National Archives)

First issued in 1932, the Silver Star is the fourth highest United States medal and is awarded to Army, Navy, and Marine personnel for "gallantry and intrepidity in action." The silver medal is suspended from a blue and white ribbon with red stripe at the center. (U.S. Army Photo)

The Legion of Merit ranks fifth in importance among medals of the United States. It is awarded for "exceptionally meritorious conduct in the performance of outstanding services." The arms of the cross are enameled white with red outline; the center is blue with white stars; the wreath behind the cross is green. The basic medal is gold and is hung from a magenta and white ribbon. (Defense Dept. Photo [Marine Corps])

Sixth in importance among United States decorations, the Distinguished Flying Cross is awarded to Army, Navy, and Marine airmen for "heroism or extraordinary achievement while participating in aerial flight." The gold medal hangs from a blue ribbon with white and red stripes. (U.S. Army Photo)

The Air Medal is ninth in importance among United States medals. The silver medal hangs from a blue ribbon with two yellow stripes and is awarded only to airmen for "meritorious achievement while participating in aerial flight." (Defense Dept. Photo [Marine Corps])

The Order of the Purple Heart was established by George Washington in 1782 and was revived in 1932. The purple and gold medal hangs from a purple and white ribbon. A profile of Washington decorates the obverse side of this medal, which is awarded to members of the armed forces who are honorably wounded in action against the enemy. (National Archives)

Index

A

aces, 47-98
 Korean war, 99-108
air-cooled engines, 2
Aircobra (see P-39)
airstrip, South Pacific, **27**
Aldrich, Donald N., 58-63, **65**
 decorations held by, 63
all-weather fighter, 18
Annie Mo, 100, **102**
Arawe, 40
armament, **4**, 5, 13, **42**
armor, 5
Arnold, Henry H. (Hap), Gen., 4
Ashmun, George M., 87
attack type F4U Corsairs, 20
AU-1, 18, **19**
Avengers (see TBF Avengers)

B

B-24 Liberator, 30, 53, 54, 82
B-25 Mitchell, 30
Baga Island, 56
Ballale, 82
Banika, 33, 34
Barinott, Beulah (see Walsh, Kenneth, wife of)
Bedford, **50**
Bernard, **78, 80**
Bettys, 72
Bismarck Archipelago, 25, **28**, 41
Blackburn's Irregulars (see VF-17)
Blackburn, John R. Lt., 89
bomber escort, 1, 30, 67
bombing raids, 1
bombs, 5, **8**, 13, 14, **43**, 45

Bonis, 30
Bookman, **80**
Bordelon, Guy P. Jr., **100, 101, 104, 105**
Bougainville, 27, 30, 30, **32**, 34-38, 47, 49, 52-54, 63, 67, 76, 86, 87, 91, 95, 97
Boyington, Gregory, 74-88, **75**
 Medal of Honor winner, 82
Brewer, **50**
Brewster Aeronautical Corp., 6
British Royal Navy F4U Corsairs, **11**
Britt, **78**
Bunker Hill, 36, 90, 91
Burnett, **78, 80**

C

"cactus air force," 30
Cannon, **50**
canopy, **9, 10**
Cape St. George, 68
Carl, Marion, 86
Carolines, 25, 44
Carpenter, Vincent, **78, 80**
carrier fighter protection, 45
carrier suitability, 12
Cavanaugh, **78, 80**
citation, VMF-111, 39
Clark, R.E., **65**
Clifton, 11
cockpit, **3, 6, 7**
color schemes, **4**
combat figures, sorties, kills, losses, 45-46
combat modifications, 10
Corsair (see F4U Corsair)
Corsair II, **11, 38, 39**
Crowe, **50**
Curran, **80**

D

Dauntless (see SBD Dauntless)
"Death Rattler" squadron, 45
Deetz, F., **65, 78, 80**
DeLeva, Ray, **87**
Devil Dogs (see VMF-111)
division leader, 109
Dunbar, **80**

E

Efate, 47
Eisele, **80**
Eldridge, William, 45
elements, 109
Ellis, **78**
Emirau, 40
Empress Augusta Bay, 35, 36, 37, 63, 67, 72, 91
English, **50**
Enterprise, 27
Espiritu Santo, 47, 49, 63, 70, 72, 76
Essex, 36, 45, 91
Ewa, 70

F

F2G-1D high-power Corsair, **23**
F3A-1, 6, **8**
F4F Wildcat, 30
  Zeroes vs., 30
F4U Corsairs, **6**
  attack type, **20**
  British use of, 12
  design and development of, 1-3
  flight tests, 8
  French Navy use of, 18
  performance statistics, flight testing, 8
  Zero vs., 10
F4U-1,**11**, 13, **36, 40, 43, 48, 83, 84, 85, 92**
F4U-4, **14**, 15, **56**
F4U-5, **15-18**, 100
F4U-6, **20**
F4U-7, 18, **22**
F6F Hellcats, 10
FG-1, 6, **12**
Fidler, **78, 80**
Fighting Corsairs (see VMF-215)
Finchhafen, 44
Finn, **50**
Fisher, Moe, 82
flak, 54
flight tests, 8
Florida Island, 33

Flying Tigers, 74, 75
formation flight, **96**
Foss, Joe, 86
Franklin, **50**
French use of F4U Corsairs, 18
fuel tanks, 3, 5
  droppable, 13

G

Gilberts, 39, 44
Gise, William, 49, **50**
Goodyear Aircraft, 6
Green Islands, 40
group, 109
Guadalcanal, 1, 25-27, 30, 33, 34, 45, 47, 52, 53, 72, 76
gull wing design, 2, 18
guns, **4**, 5, 13, **42**

H

Halsey, William F. (Bull), Adm., 30
Hamilton-Standard propellers, 2
Hansen, Herman, 76
Hanson, Robert M.,**60**, 66-68
  Medal of Honor winner, 68
Hartsock, **50**
Hart, **50**
Hatch, **80**
Hawaii, 61
Hazelwood, **78, 80**
Hedrick, Roger, Lt., 91
Helena, 101
Hellcats (see F6F)
Hernan, **80**
high-altitude fighter, **22**
Hiyo, 33
Hollmeyer, **78, 80**
Hoover, **78**
Hornet, 27
Hospers, Jack, 12
Hunter, **80**

I

I Operation, 33
Independence, 36
Iwo Jima, 42, 45

J

Japan home islands, 45
Jensen, **80**
Johnston, **50**
Junyo, 33

K

Kahili, 30, 35, 52-54, 80, 82
Kamikaze attacks, 45
Kara, 30
Kaseman, **50**
Kates, 67
Kavieng, 86
Kepford, Ira C., 87-97, **89**
Kieta, 30
kills, 45, 48, 49
Kimpo, 99, 101
Klingman, Robert, 45, **46**
Knipping, **80**
Koga, Mineichi, Adm., 34, 35, 38, 43
Kolombangara, 35, 72
Korean war, 15, 18, 99-108
Kraft, **78**
Kuhn, **50**

L

LA-11 fighters, 104
Lae, 44
Lakunai, 26
Lamger, **50**
landing gear, 3, **37**, **44**
  carrier problems and, 12
Lanphier, **78**
leaders, 109
Liberator (see B-24)
Lightning (see P-38)
Lindbergh, Charles A., 13
liquid-cooled engines, 2, 5
losses, 45
Love Day operation, 36
Loyalty Islands, 49
Lurline, 76
Luthi, **78**

M

MacArthur, Douglas, Gen., 25, 40, 44
MAG-11, 70
Magda, John, 11
Marianas, 43, 44
Marianas Turkey Shoot, 43
Marshalls, 39, 44
McCall, D.E., **65, 80**
McDowell, **50**
McQueen, Don, Ens., 91
Medal of Honor
  Boyington, Gregory, 82
  Hanson, Robert, 68
  Walsh, Kenneth, 53, 58
Merrit, Lewis G., Maj. Gen., 68

Midway, 61, 70
Miller, W. Howard, **41, 78, 80**
Mitchell (see B-25)
Mitchell, Ralph, Gen., 83
Moak, D.R., **65, 80**
modifications, combat, 10
Munda, 34, 35, 44, **52**-56, 63, 72, 77, 82
Mutz, **50**

N

napalm, **44**, 45
Neefus, J.L., **65**
New Britain, 25, 34, 40, 63, 74
New Caledonia, 49, 76
New Georgia, 34, 36, 52, 70, 72, 90
New Guinea, 25, 36, 44
New Hebrides, 47, 49, 72, 76
New Ireland, 86
Newman, **50**
night fighter, 7, 18, 44, 99-108
night flying maneuvers, 10
Nimitz, Chester, Adm., 25, 27, 44
North Island, 10
Noumea, 76

O

O'Dell, B.P., **65, 78, 80**
O'Hare, Butch, 10
Okinawa, 42, 45, 56, 58
Ole 122, **40, 41**
oleo struts, 12
Operation Bed Check Charlie, 99, 101, 104
organizations, 109-116
Owens, Robert G., **65**, 80

P

P-38 Lightning, 1, 2, 10, 30, 34, 52, 82
P-39 Aircobra, 10, 30, 53, 82
P-40 Warhawk, 1, 30, 34, 52, 53, 56, 75
P-47, 10
P-51, 10
Pace, William H., **78**
Pacific Theater of Operations, **26**
Palau, **44**
Pearson, **50**
Pettit, **78, 80**
Philippines, 25, 44, 58
Pierce, F.E., Col., **73**
Piva, 38, 91
Porter, Sam, 8
powerplants, 2, **13**, 15
  air- vs. liquid-cooled, 2, 5
  supercharging, 7

Pratt and Whitney engines, 2, 4
Princeton, 37, 100, 101, 104
production engineering, 6
production models, 5
Project Dog, 12
propeller, 2
　used as weapon, 45, **46**
prototype, **2**

Q

Quilty, **50**

R

Rabaul (see Solomons-Rabaul area)
radar, 14
Ranger, 49
Rankin, David, **78, 80**
Rapopo, 26
Raymond, **50**
Rendova, 34, 35, 69, 70, 72
Rickenbaker, Eddie, 86
Ridderhoff, Stanley, Col., 10
Rood, **50**
Roosevelt, Franklin D., **53**, 58
Ross, Harry, **55**
rotation, 47
Royal New Zealand Air Force, **38**
Rufe seaplane, 95
Russells, 33, 34, 53, 70, 77

S

Saigon, 45
Saipan, 43
Samoa, 70
Santa Cruz, 27
Saratoga, 27, 37
SBD Dauntless, 30, 77
Scarborough, **78, 80**
Schaefer, **78**
search radar, 14, 101
Segal, Harold E., 71-74, **73**
Shelton, **50**
Sigel, **78, 80**
Simpson Harbor, **34**, 41, 67
Slot, The, 1, 33, 34
Smith, Fred, **41**
snipers, 48
Solomons-Rabaul area, 1, 25-27, 30, **31**,
　33-44, 47, 48, 49, 53, 58, 61, 63, 67-69,
　72-74, 83, 86, 87, 91
sorties, 45
Spears, Harold L., **60**, 63-65
speed testing, 4
Spencer, W.P., **50**, 54

squadron histories, 109-116
St. George's Channel, 68, 86, 87
St. Valentine's Day Massacre, Solomons, 30,
　52
Stidger, C.S., **65**
Sundowners (see VF-11)
supercharger, 7, 18
Swashbucklers (see VMF-214)
"Sweetheart of Okinawa," 45
Synar, **80**

T

Tarawa, 42
Taylor, **50, 80**
TBF Avengers, 30, 68
Tenekow, 30
Thomas, Wilbur J., 68-71, **69**
Tobero, 26
Tojos, 96
Tokyo, 45
Tomahawks (see P-40)
Tomlinson, T.M., **65, 80**
Tonys, 86
Torokina, 30, **33**, 35, 37, 38, 63, 67
Towers, John, Adm., 4
Truk, 25, 34, 40, 41, 44
Turbo-Engineering Co., 7

V

Val dive bombers, 33, 52, 53
Vanguna, 34, 69, 70
VC-3 squadron, 100
Vella Lavella, 35, 36, 47, 52, 56, 63, **66**, 67,
　83
　decorations presentation ceremony, **65**
VF(N)-101, 44
VF(N)-75, 44
VF-11 "Sundowners," 101
VF-12 squadron, 10
VF-17, 49, 72, 87
　formation flight, **96**
　markings, **92**
VF-301 squadron, 12
visibility, 3
VMF-111 "Devil Dogs," 39, 40
VMF-112 "Wolf Pack," 77, 110
VMF-115, 74
VMF-121, 34, 35, 110
VMF-122, 34, 35, 48, **76-77**, 110
VMF-123, 53, 111
VMF-124, 10, 30, 34, 45, 48, 49, **50**, 70, 111
VMF-211, **36**, 48, 112
VMF-212, 48, 112
VMF-213, 33, 34, 35, 48, 68

VMF-214, 33, 48, 77, **78**, 82
  F4U-1 of, **83-85**
VMF-215 "Fighting Corsairs," 48, 58, 63, 66
VMF-221, 33, 35, 48, 71, 73
VMF-222, 58
VMF-462, 65
VMR-152, 58
Vought, Chance, 2, 6, 12, 14
Vunakanau, 26

W

Walsh, Kenneth, **48**, 49-58
  decorations held by, 58
  kills accredited to, 55
  Medal of Honor winner, 53, 58
Warhawk (see P-40)
"Washing Machine Charlie," 44
Wasp, 27, 49
"Whistling Death, The," 33, **37**
Wildcats (see F4F)
Williams, O. Keith, **65**
Williamson, H.H., **65**

Williams, **78, 80**
wingman, 109
wings, 109
wings (see gull wing design)
Wolf Pack (see VMF-112)
Wotje Atoll, 13

X

XF4U-1, **3, 5**

Y

YAK-18 monoplanes, 104
Yamamoto, Isoroku, Adm., 33, 34
Yorktown, 49, 106

Z

Zeroes, 1, 33-35, 45, 47, **52**-56, 61-63, 67-72, 87, 96, 97
  F4F Wildcat vs., 30
  F4U Corsairs vs., 10
Zuiho, 33
Zuikaku, 33